# BASIC ENGLISH GRAMMAR

## BOOK-1

(INTERNATIONAL EDITION)

(With Clear-cut Explanations of Grammatical Rules)

T. R. Bhanot

**DREAMLAND PUBLICATIONS**
J-128, Kirti Nagar, New Delhi -110 015, India
Phone : +91-11-2510 6050, 2543 5657
E-mail : dreamland@dreamlandpublications.com
Shop online at www.dreamlandpublications.com
Follow us on www.instagram.com/dreamland.publications

Published 2024 by
**DREAMLAND PUBLICATIONS**
J-128, Kirti Nagar, New Delhi - 110 015, India
Tel : +91-11-2510 6050, 2543 5657
E-mail : dreamland@dreamlandpublications.com
www.dreamlandpublications.com

Printed in India

---

# PREFACE

Grammar is the most essential tool for learning a language in its correct form. Currently, there is a flood of books on grammar in the market, yet most of them are mere collections of examples and exercises with no cohesive structure to guide learners from beginning to end. Evidently, they fail to achieve the intended purpose of a grammar book.

Dreamland Publications presents a series of seven books titled '**Basic English Grammar**,' which offers clear and simple explanations of the rules of English grammar. Each book contains lessons followed by exercises that encourage students to demonstrate their understanding of the topics covered in the book.

With clear and concise definitions, examples, and practice exercises, this series serves as a valuable tool for all students looking to improve their grammatical skills.

—**PUBLISHERS**

# ABOUT THE BOOK

**BASIC ENGLISH GRAMMAR** is a series of seven books designed for students in the primary and middle classes. It stands out as a series with a difference, as it presents the subject matter in a properly graded manner. Furthermore, it covers the latest developments in English Grammar in an easy-to-understand style.

The present book is the second installment in the series and is intended for beginners in the realm of grammar instruction. Fundamental concepts are presented and explained using pictures and examples, ensuring that young learners encounter no difficulty in grasping the basics.

The most outstanding feature of the series is the structure of the practice exercises at the end of each chapter. Each exercise is divided into two main parts: **CLASSWORK** and **HOMEWORK**. Additionally, ample space is provided in the book for students to solve each question directly on its pages.

I am delighted to present this series to English language teachers, hoping that it will serve its intended purpose admirably. Let the series speak for itself and establish its reputation based on its strengths compared to other books on the subject.

*Originality and perfection reside solely with the Almighty.* Every human endeavour, however efficient, inevitably leaves room for improvement. Therefore, constructive suggestions for enhancing the series are warmly welcomed. No effort will be spared to incorporate truly valuable suggestions into subsequent editions of the series.

**—AUTHOR**

# CONTENTS

**I—APPLIED GRAMMAR .................. 5-100**

1. Sounds and Letters .................. 5
2. Capital and Small Letters .................. 8
3. Vowels and Consonants .................. 12
4. Words .................. 16
5. Sentences .................. 20
6. Speech and Its Parts .................. 24
7. Nouns .................. 27
8. Pronouns .................. 31
9. The Number .................. 36
10. The Gender .................. 43
11. The Person .................. 50
12. Determiners : A, An, The .................. 56
13. Possessive Words .................. 60
14. Demonstrative Words .................. 65
15. Adjectives .................. 70
16. Verbs .................. 75
17. Adverbs .................. 80
18. Prepositions .................. 85
19. Conjunctions .................. 91
20. Interjections .................. 95
21. Parsing .................. 98
22. Questions and Answers .................. 99

**II—VOCABULARY .................. 101**

Days of the Week, Months of the Year, Subjects, Games and Sports, Cries of Animals and Their Young Ones, Homes, Meals, Occupations, Things Where Made, Things Where Kept, Games Where Played, Smaller Pieces, Common Diseases, Words Written Together, Words Written Separately, Avoid These Pitfalls, Common Phrases, Common Proverbs, A Crossword Puzzle.

**III—SPELLING AND PRONUNCIATION .................. 108**

**IV—WRITTEN COMPOSITION .................. 111-120**

Essay-Writing .................. 111

Story-Writing .................. 115

Application-Writing .................. 119

# SECTION I — APPLIED GRAMMAR

## Lesson 1 : Sounds and Letters

**OBJECTIVES**

To enable the pupils to—

- know the difference between a sound and a letter.
- know the order of letters in the English Alphabet.
- know the number of letters used in English.
- identify the sound of the first letter of a word.

**FACTS AND RULES**

- We use the following 26 letters of the alphabet (from a to z) in all, to read and write English :
  A, B, C, D, E, F, G, H, I, J, K, L, M, N, O, P, Q, R, S, T, U, V, W, X,Y, Z
- Each letter of the English alphabet stands for a certain sound.
- Letters of the English alphabet are always written in a certain order.
- After seeing a letter, we think of its sound and speak it.

Recall your first lesson in the English language in your Nursery Standard. Your teacher taught you some sounds:

A for APPLE

M for MAN

S for SOAP

Z for ZEBRA

How many sounds did you learn? Do you remember? You learnt 26 sounds in all, from A to Z. These 26 sounds helped you to speak English words.

### THE LETTERS

Later on, you learnt how to write each sound through a **symbol**. So you came to have 26 symbols for writing English. They are —

**A B C D E F G H I J K L M N O P Q**
**R S T U V W X Y Z**

Each of these sound-symbols is called a **letter**. So there are 26 letters in all in the English language.

**A letter is a symbol used for writing a certain sound.**

**The set of 26 letters used to write English is called the alphabet.**

The letters of the alphabet are written in a certain order as given above.

## CLASSWORK

I. *Write the 26 letters of the English Alphabet:*

........ ........ ........ ........ ........ ........ ........

........ ........ ........ ........ ........ ........ ........

........ ........ ........ ........ ........ ........ ........

........ ........ ........ ........ ........

II. *Fill in the blanks:*

1. We use..................................................basic sounds to speak English.
2. We use 26...............................................................to write English.
3. The English alphabet is a...................................................of 26 letters.
4. Sounds are...............................................................................orally.
5. Each speaking sound has a..................................................for writing it.
6. Each sound-symbol is called a...............................................................
7. Letters are used both for..................................and ...............................
8. The English alphabet starts with the letter ...............................................
9. The English alphabet ends with the letter ..................................................
10. Sounds are used for.................................... , not for...............................
11. We started learning basic English sounds in our...........................Standard.
12. We learnt................................................. basic English sounds in all.
    These sounds helped us to.....................................................English.

III. *Answer* **yes** *or* **no**:

1. Do we have 35 letters in English? ..........................
2. Does D come before C in the alphabet? ..........................
3. Does H come after G in the alphabet? ..........................
4. Have we 26 basic sounds in English? ..........................
5. Has each sound a symbol for writing it? ..........................

## HOMEWORK

IV. *Answer the following questions:*

1. How many basic sounds do we use in English? ....................................
2. How many letters do we use in English? ....................................
3. Which is the first letter of the English alphabet? ....................................
4. Which is the last letter of the English alphabet? ....................................
5. Which letters come before and after D? ............... , ...............
6. Which letters come after and before R? ............... , ...............
7. Which letter comes between L and N? ....................................
8. Which is the 8th letter in the English alphabet? ....................................
9. Which is the 20th letter in the English alphabet? ....................................
10. Which letter comes before L and after J? ....................................
11. Which English letter is like a circle in shape? ....................................

V. *What is a* **letter**?

..............................................................................................................................

..............................................................................................................................

VI. *What is the* **English Alphabet**?

..............................................................................................................................

..............................................................................................................................

VII. *Here are four pictures. Write the first letter of the word for each picture:*

# Lesson 2 : Capital and Small Letters

## OBJECTIVES

To enable the pupils to know that—

- English letters are written in two forms.
- know the order of letters in the English Alphabet.
- the letters in large form are called capitals.
- capital letters are used according to certain rules.

## FACTS AND RULES

- The first letter of a particular name is always capital, as: Peter, London, Taj Mahal.
- The first word of a sentence begins with a capital letter, as: The cow is a milch animal.
- Letter I and O when written alone are always capital, as: I am a student. Save me, O God.
- An abbreviation is written in capital letters, as: Prime Minister ▶ P.M., Station Master ▶ S.M.
- The first word of each line in poetry begins with a capital letter, as:

Do what you do,
With all your might;
Things done by halves,
Are never done right.

A,B,C,
Tumbled down D;
Cat is in the cupboard,
It can't see me.

Twinkle, twinkle, little star!
How I wonder what you are;
Up above the world so high,
Like a diamond in the sky.

## TWO FORMS OF LETTERS

You have learnt that 26 letters are used for writing English. Each of these letters can be written in two forms, as:

1. A,a 2. B,b 3. C,c 4. D,d 5. E,e

So the English alphabet can be written in two forms:

| A | B | C | D | E | F | G | H | I | J |
|---|---|---|---|---|---|---|---|---|---|
| K | L | M | N | O | P | Q | R | S | T |
| | | U | V | W | X | Y | Z | | |

| a | b | c | d | e | f | g | h | i | j |
|---|---|---|---|---|---|---|---|---|---|
| k | l | m | n | o | p | q | r | s | t |
| | | u | v | w | x | y | z | | |

## CAPITAL LETTERS

Observe the two forms of the letters given above. The form on the left is larger than that on the right.

English letters written in the large form are called **capital letters** or **capitals,** as : A, B, C, D.............

## SMALL LETTERS

The form of letters given on the right is smaller. English letters in the smaller form are called **small letters** or **smalls**; as: a, b, c, d.......

Both these forms of letters are used while writing English. However, in speaking, these forms are not there. The small letters find much more use in writing than the capital letters.

## USE OF CAPITAL LETTERS

As mentioned above, writing in English is done mostly through small letters. Capital letters are used here and there only. But without their use, the writing becomes incorrect. Let us learn where to use the capital letters:

1. *The first letter of a particular name is always capital, as:*

   Peter    Maria    Monday    Paris
   India    God    Oxford Street    Japanese
   Jupiter    Bible    Tim    Jade

2. *The first letter of the first word of a sentence is always capital, as:*

   1. My name is Susan.    2. He is an honest man.

3. *Letters I, O, when written alone, are always capital, as:*

   1. You are a boy but I am a girl.
   2. Save me, O God, from sin.

4. *The first letter of the first word of each line in poetry is capital, as:*

   Work while you work,
   And play while you play;
   This is the best rule,
   To be healthy and gay.

5. Letters used to write complete words in short form are capital, *as:*

   1. M.O. for *Money Order*    2. P.O. for *Post Office*
   3. S.M. for *Station Master*    4. S.I. for *Sub-Inspector*
   5. S.P.O. for *Special Police Officer*

# Practice Exercises

## CLASSWORK

I. *Write the English alphabet in* **capital letters***:*

........ ........ ........ ........ ........ ........ ........

........ ........ ........ ........ ........ ........ ........

........ ........ ........ ........ ........ ........ ........

........ ........ ........ ........ ........

II. *Write the English alphabet in* **small letters***:*

........ ........ ........ ........ ........ ........ ........

........ ........ ........ ........ ........ ........ ........

........ ........ ........ ........ ........ ........ ........

........ ........ ........ ........ ........

III. *Here is a list of words. Six of these words must begin with* **capital letters***. Sort them out and write below*:

| table | jane | roof | europe | teacher | april |
|---|---|---|---|---|---|
| pencil | friday | france | chair | london | wall |

............................ ............................ ............................

............................ ............................ ............................

## HOMEWORK

IV. *Write the following in* **short form***:*

1. Prime Minister ............................
2. Please Turn Over ............................
3. Station House Officer ............................
4. Railway Mail Service ............................
5. General Post Office ............................
6. Money Order ............................

V. *Rewrite each sentence using* **capital letters** *wherever necessary:*

1. my father is a doctor.

   ..........................................................................................

2. tom will tell us a story.

   ..........................................................................................

3. the thames flows through london.

   ..........................................................................................

4. i am innocent, o god.

   ..........................................................................................

5. all work and no play,
   makes jack a murky boy;
   all play and no work,
   makes him a shirky boy.

   ..........................................................................................

   ..........................................................................................

   ..........................................................................................

   ..........................................................................................

VI. *Fill in the blanks:*

1. Letters in large form are called ..........................................
2. Letters in small form are called ..........................................
3. Letters .................. , ..................... , when written alone, are always capital.
4. The first letter of each particular .......................................... is capital.
5. The first letter of the first word of each ................................ is capital.

VII. *Name the* **two forms** *of English letters:*

1. ................................................ 2. ................................................

# Lesson 3 : Vowels and Consonants

## OBJECTIVES

To enable the pupils to know that —

- vowels are sounds/letters spoken with unstopped breath in the mouth.
- consonants are sounds/letters spoken with stopped breath in the mouth.
- there are 5 vowels ( a, e, i. o, u ) and 21 consonants: ( b, c, d, f, g, h, j, k, l, m, n, p, q, r, s, t, v, w, x, y, z )

## FACTS AND RULES

- Vowels are the soul of the English language as without them it is impossible to speak English.
- Consonants make a sound only when they are combined with vowels.
- We cannot speak combined consonants properly, unless they combine with vowels also, as:

| Vowel A | | | Vowel E | | | Vowel I | | | Vowel O | | | Vowel U | | |
|---|---|---|---|---|---|---|---|---|---|---|---|---|---|---|
| C↑T | M↑N | Y↑K | B↑D | H↑N | P↑T | B↑B | L↑P | P↑T | D↑G | H↑T | T↑P | C↑P | S↑N | T↑B |
| A | A | A | E | E | E | I | I | I | O | O | O | U | U | U |
| CAT | MAN | YAK | BED | HEN | PET | BIB | LIP | PIT | DOG | HOT | TOP | CUP | SUN | TUB |

## OPEN AND CLOSED SOUNDS

We use 26 basic sounds in English. Speak a few of them orally. While speaking some of them, breath comes out freely. We do not shut our mouth completely. Nor does our tongue stop the breath. Such sounds are only five in number. They are **a,e,i,o,u.**

While speaking these five sounds, breath does not stop anywhere and the mouth remains open. In other words, it is the *open breath* that makes these sounds. So these five sounds are called **open sounds**.

But while speaking the other 21 sounds, breath does not come out freely. We have to either shut our mouth or use the tongue to stop the breath. These sounds are **b, c, d, f, g, h, j, k, l, m, n, p, q, r, s t, v, w, x, y, z**.

Breath is once stopped and then released while speaking these sounds. In other words, it is the *closed breath* that makes these sounds. So they are called **closed sounds**.

## VOWELS OR SONANTS

Five open sounds of **a, e, i, o, u** are called **vowels** or **sonants**. **Vowels are open sounds that can be spoken freely.**

Vowels are the most important sounds. They are the very soul of the English language. Without them, it is just impossible to speak English. Read a full page of your reader. You won't find even a single word that is without a vowel sound.

## NON-VOWELS OR CONSONANTS

The remaining 21 sounds are called **non-vowels** or **consonants**.

Consonants cannot be spoken freely until and unless they combine with vowels. They sound properly in their company only. So they are called **consonants**.

**Consonants are closed sounds that can be properly spoken only when they combine with vowels.**

26 SOUNDS (*a* to *z*)

*Vowels (5)*
*a, e, i, o, u*

*Consonants (21)*
*b, c, d, f, g, h, j, k, j, m, n*
*p, q, r, s, t, v, w, x, y, z*

Take two consonants **p**, **t** and combine them as **pt**, we cannot speak them properly. Insert between them the five vowels in turn. We shall get five words:

| P T | P T | P T | P T | P T |
|---|---|---|---|---|
| *a* | *e* | *i* | *0* | *u* |
| **Pat** | **Pet** | **Pit** | **Pot** | **Put** |

We can pronounce these words easily and properly.

Similar is the case with **pll**:

| P LL | P LL | P LL | P LL | P LL |
|---|---|---|---|---|
| *a* | *e* | *i* | *0* | *u* |
| **Pall** | **Pell** | **Pill** | **Poll** | **Pull** |

# Practice Exercises

## CLASSWORK

I. *Put a circle round each* **vowel***:*

h a i g z w e x r d f

o c p i b y v u j s e

II. *Put a circle round* each **consonant**:

a i o e b u i p e z

III. *Fill in the blanks with a* **vowel** *to complete each word:*

| | | | | | |
|---|---|---|---|---|---|
| 1. | b........t | 2. | b........x | 3. | b........g |
| 4. | b........y | 5. | ........nt | 6. | ar........ |
| 7. | ........gg | 8. | ........ff | 9. | f........n |
| 10. | f........r | 11. | ........at | 12. | j........g |

IV. *Fill in the blanks with a* **consonant** *to complete each word:*

| | | | | | |
|---|---|---|---|---|---|
| 1. | ........an | 2. | ga........e | 3. | pla........e |
| 4. | ........all | 5. | ca........e | 6. | ar........ |
| 7. | f........y | 8. | ........uy | 9. | to........ |
| 10. | wal........ | 11. | tra........ | 12. | a........d |

V. *Fill in the blanks:*

1. We have..........................................................open sounds in English.
2. We have.......................................................closed sounds in English.
3. Consonants don't sound unless they....................................with vowels.
4. Our breath comes out........................................while speaking vowels.
5. Consonants are called..........................................................................also.
6. Vowels are...................... sounds while ................ are closed sounds.
7. Our breath once.........and then comes out while speaking a consonant.

## HOMEWORK

VI. *What are* **vowels***? How many are they in all?*

..............................................................................................................................................................

..............................................................................................................................................................

VII. *What are* **consonants***? How many are they in all?*

..............................................................................................................................................................

..............................................................................................................................................................

VIII. *Write* **five words** *beginning with each vowel:*

| *a* | *e* | *i* | *o* | *u* |
|---|---|---|---|---|
| ............ | ............ | ............ | ............ | ............ |
| ............ | ............ | ............ | ............ | ............ |
| ............ | ............ | ............ | ............ | ............ |
| ............ | ............ | ............ | ............ | ............ |
| ............ | ............ | ............ | ............ | ............ |

IX. *Sort out* **vowels** *and* **consonants** *in each word and write them in their columns:*

| | Word | Vowels | Consonants |
|---|---|---|---|
| 1. | queue | ............................ | .......................................... |
| 2. | soup | ............................ | .......................................... |
| 3. | slow | ............................ | .......................................... |
| 4. | supply | ............................ | .......................................... |
| 5. | bazaar | ............................ | .......................................... |
| 6. | eel | ............................ | .......................................... |
| 7. | fuel | ............................ | .......................................... |
| 8. | special | ............................ | .......................................... |
| 9. | cream | ............................ | .......................................... |

# Lesson 4 : Words

## OBJECTIVES

To enable the pupils to know that —

- sounds combine to form spoken words.
- letters combine to form written words.
- a word is a group of sounds or letters that has meaning.
- words are the basic units of a language.

## FACTS AND RULES

- Sounds of the letters *a, n, t* combine to form the spoken word **ant**.
- Letters *a, n, t* combine to form the written word **ant**.
- Each word points to or gives an idea of something — a *name*, a *fact*, a *quality*, a *feeling* or an *action*, as :

  1. The word—*John*—points to a *person*.
  2. The word—*black*—points to a *colour*.
  3. The word—*active*—points to a *quality*.
  4. The word—*read*—points to an *action*.
  5. The word—*alas!*—points to a *feeling*.
  6. The word—*sunrise*—points to a *fact*.

- In order to express a thought, several words are spoken or written in a certain order.
- Each language is like a building while its words are like *bricks*.
- Consonants can't make words on their own. They combine with vowels to do so.

## THE SEEDS

Sounds/letters are the seeds of a language. They combine to form **words**.

*Let us study some examples:*

1. The sounds of a, n, t combine to form the spoken word — **ant**.
2. The letters b, o, x combine to form the written word — **box**.

We see that sounds or letters combine in different ways to form different words. Each word has its own meaning as well.

**A word is a sound/letter or a set of sounds/letters that has meaning.**

Different words have different meanings. Some words stand for persons, animals or places. Others point to actions or qualities. Still others show the feelings of the heart, as :

1. The word—Sam—names a *person*.
2. The word—room—names a *place*.
3. The word—chair—names an *object*.
4. The word—good—stands for a *quality*.
5. The word—runs—indicates an *action*.
6. The word—hurrah!—shows the *feeling of joy*.

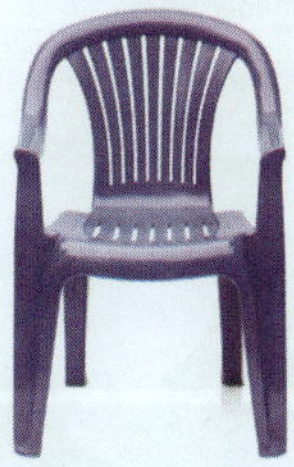

## THE BASIC UNIT

*Word* is the **basic unit** of a language. Each word has a meaning to express, the *name* of a *person*, a *place*, a *thing*, a *fact*, a *quality*, an *action* or a *sudden feeling*.

When a number of words are put together in a proper order, they make a **sentence**. And when we speak or write a number of sentences in a proper order, we speak or write a *language*.

**Words are like bricks that are used to build up a language.**

So one must learn a good storehouse of the words of a language in order to speak or write it properly.

**Remember that—**

- consonants cannot make words by themselves. They must combine with vowels to do so.
- each word creates an idea of something in the mind. But a sentence joins these ideas to form a complete thought.

# Practice Exercises

## CLASSWORK

I. *Make a* **word** *with each set of letters:*

| | | | |
|---|---|---|---|
| 1. c, r, y | ........................ | 2. p, a, g, e | ........................ |
| 3. f, o, x | ........................ | 4. e, a, t, s | ........................ |
| 5. w, a, s | ........................ | 6. y, e, a, r | ........................ |

II. *Write the* **word** *for each picture given below:*

.............................. .............................. ..............................

III. *Arrange each set of letters in proper order to make a* **word** *from it. One is done for you:*

| | | |
|---|---|---|
| 1. t, n, r, i, a | t, r, a, i, n | train |
| 2. a, l, p, e, p | ............................ | ........................ |
| 3. y, g, u, l | ............................ | ........................ |
| 4. l, s, o, c, h, o | ............................ | ........................ |
| 5. e, h, u, o, s | ............................ | ........................ |
| 6. r, g, a, g, e, b | ............................ | ........................ |
| 7. d, e, r, a, l, e | ............................ | ........................ |
| 8. p, s, e, c, e, h | ............................ | ........................ |

## HOMEWORK

IV. *Each set of letters can make* **two words**. *One of them is given. Write the other:*

1. a, s, w — was — ............................
2. e, a, d, r — read — ............................
3. r, a, e, n — earn — ............................
4. p, e, w, e, s — weeps — ............................
5. r, a, l, i — rail — ............................
6. r, p, a, e — reap — ............................

V. *Make* **two words** *from each set of letters:*

1. e, p, c, a, h — ............................ — ............................
2. n, o, w — ............................ — ............................
3. e, s, a, t, t — ............................ — ............................
4. c, t, a, e, h — ............................ — ............................
5. w, f, o, l — ............................ — ............................
6. n, e, o, t — ............................ — ............................

VI. *Fill in each blank with a suitable word:*

1. Sounds/letters are the........................................................of a language.
2. Words are like......................................................used to build up a language.
3. One must have a good........................................................................of words.
4. Consonants cannot make...............................without combining with vowels.
5. Each word has a.......................................................to express something.
6. Words put in a proper order make a.....................................................
7. Sentences put in a proper order make a...............................................

VII. *What is a* **word**?

....................................................................................................................................

....................................................................................................................................

# Lesson 5 : Sentences

## OBJECTIVES

To enable the pupils to know that —

- single words give/point to separate ideas only.
- when words combine in a proper order, they make sentences.
- a sentence forms a complete thought in the mind.
- words not combining in a proper order make no sense.

## FACTS AND RULES

- A single word points to just an idea of something, as:
  1. The word—*Jade*—gives an idea of a *person's name*.
  2. The word—*eats*—gives an idea of an *action* only.
  3. The word—*food*—gives an idea of an *eatable* only.
- Words set in a proper order combine their separate ideas to form a meaningful thought, as:
  1. *Jade eats food.*

     These three words set in this order form a meaningful fact that *a boy, named Jade, eats food*.
- If words are set in an improper order, they form no fact or thought at all, as:

  Eats Jade food<br>Food eats Jade<br>Food Jade eats<br>Eats food Jade — None of these word-sets makes any sense at all.
- A sentence is a set of words set in a proper order to express a complete thought.

We know that sounds/letters combine to make **words**. A word gives the idea of a single person, place, thing, quality, action, fact, feeling, etc. But when words combine in a proper order, they make **complete thoughts**.

*Observe the following*:

1. When we say—*Tom*, we mean a **person**.
2. When we say—*kicks*, we mean an **action**.
3. When we say—*a ball*, we mean a **thing**.

These words, taken separately, form separate ideas in the mind. Let us combine them as follows and then read:

*Tom kicks a ball.*

When we read these three words in the order given above, a **complete fact/thought** is formed in the mind. It is the result of placing these words in a *proper order*. Without this order, no complete fact or thought can be there in the mind.

For example, if we say—

*Kicks a ball Tom,* *or*

*A ball kicks Tom,* *or*

*Kicks Tom a ball,*

no complete fact or thought shall be formed in the mind.

So words must be placed in a proper order to have a clear and complete meaning. If the words are not placed in a proper order, they shall not make any sense at all.

Remember that words make a **sentence** only when they are placed in a proper order, and a **sentence** always expresses a complete thought.

**A sentence is a group of words set in a proper order to express a complete fact or thought.**

**Remember that a sentence can —**

*(a)* state a *fact* or *thought*.

*(b)* ask a *question*.

*(c)* express some *advice*, *command*, *request*, etc.

*(d)* express a *sudden feeling*.

*(e)* express a *wish* or *blessing*.

So sentences are of five kinds.

# Practice Exercises

## CLASSWORK

I. *Put each* **word** *under its picture:*

boat　　shirt　　fox　　girl

........................　........................　........................　........................

II. *Put each* **sentence** *under its picture:*

1. The cat is lapping milk.
2. The cow is grazing grass.

..............................................　..............................................

III. *Look at each picture and write a* **sentence** *for it:*

..............................................　..............................................

## HOMEWORK

IV. *Put each set of words in proper order to make a* **sentence**. *Use* **capital letters** *where necessary:*

1. a, peter, is, boy, clever

   ..................................................................................................................................

2. at, the, man, old, they, laughed

   ..................................................................................................................................

3. foot, school, come, on, i, to

   ..................................................................................................................................

4. smith, our, mr, is, principal

   ..................................................................................................................................

5. agra, to, yesterday, went, he

   ..................................................................................................................................

6. must, you, your, elders, respect

   ..................................................................................................................................

7. is, sam's, jane, wife

   ..................................................................................................................................

8. the, speak, always, truth

   ..................................................................................................................................

9. father, is, doctor, a, his

   ..................................................................................................................................

V. *What is a* **sentence**? *Give an example:*

..................................................................................................................................

..................................................................................................................................

*Example*: ..................................................................................................................

# Lesson 6 : Speech and Its Parts

## OBJECTIVES

To enable the pupils to know that—

- whatever we speak/write is our speech.
- each word in speech does a certain job.
- words have been given names according to their jobs.
- these names are called parts of speech.
- there are nine different parts of speech.

## FACTS AND RULES

- Words do nine types of jobs in speech.
- So there are nine classes of words as under:

1. Nouns—words that name things.
2. Pronouns—words used in place of nouns.
3. Determiners—words that show the reference made by nouns/pronouns.
4. Adjectives—words that qualify nouns/pronouns.
5. Verbs—words showing actions, facts or events.
6. Adverbs—words that qualify verbs, adjectives and other adverbs.
7. Prepositions—words that relate nouns/pronouns in the same sentence.
8. Conjunctions—words that join words, phrases and sentences.
9. Interjections—words that express sudden feelings.

## SPEECH

We have a natural urge to express our ideas to others. So we speak words and sentences. They form our **speech**.

**Speech means whatever we speak/write.**

## PARTS OF SPEECH

*Observe the following sentence:*

**A good child learns its lessons well.**

1. **A** stands for *numeral 1* or *any*.
2. **good**—stands for a *quality*.
3. **child**—stands for a *person*.

4. **learns**—shows an *action*.
5. **its**—shows a *relation*.
6. **lessons**—stands for *things*.
7. **well**—shows the *manner of the action*.

We see that words do different jobs in a sentence. Some words name persons, places or things. Others stand for qualities, actions and feelings. Still others do the job of linking the words in proper order. According to these jobs, words have nine classes:

1. **Nouns**—naming words
2. **Pronouns**—words used in place of nouns
3. **Determiners**—words that determine nouns
4. **Adjectives**—words qualifying nouns or pronouns
5. **Verbs**—words showing actions
6. **Adverbs**—words that qualify verbs or adjectives
7. **Prepositions**—words relating nouns and pronouns in a sentence
8. **Conjunctions**—words joining words or sentences
9. **Interjections**—words that express sudden feelings/emotions

**These nine classes of words are called** *parts of speech*.

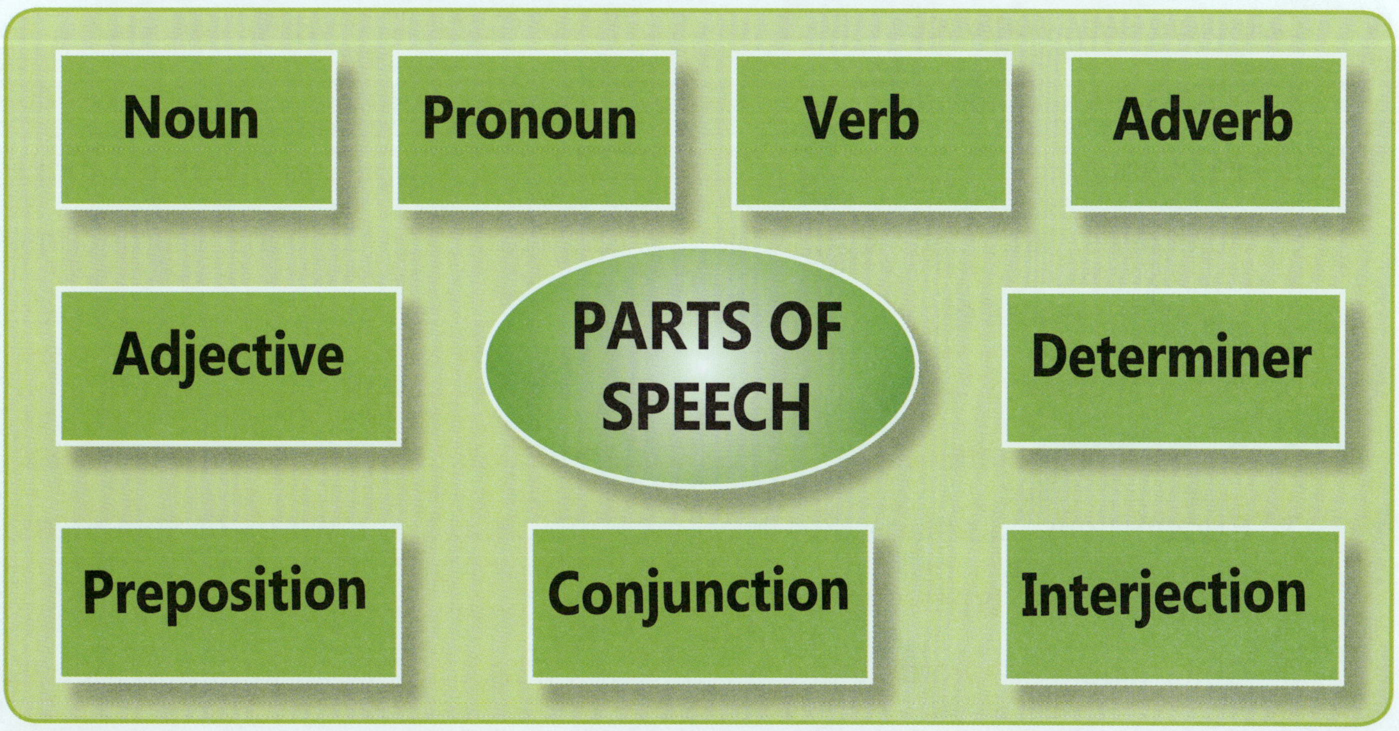

# Practice Exercises

## CLASSWORK

I. *What do you mean by* **speech***?*

..........................................................................................................................

II. *Name the* **nine classes** *of words:*

| | | |
|---|---|---|
| 1. ........................ | 2. ...................... | 3. ...................... |
| 4. ....................... | 5. ...................... | 6. ...................... |
| 7. ....................... | 8. ...................... | 9. ...................... |

III. *Fill in each blank with a suitable word*:

1. We have a natural.............................................................................to speak.
2. We want to.....................................................................................our ideas.
3. Each word does a..............................................................job in a sentence.
4. Nine classes of words are called...................................................................

## HOMEWORK

IV. *Complete each sentence:*

1. Nouns are..........................................................................................words.
2. We want to..........................................................................our ideas to others.
3. Adjectives.........................................................................nouns or pronouns.
4. Verbs are words of ..........................................................................................
5. Adverbs qualify............................., ............................or .............................
6. Prepositions relate.............................and...............................in a sentence.
7. Conjunctions.........................................................................words or sentences.
8. Interjections express sudden...........................................................................
9. Determiners are words that.................................................................nouns.

# Lesson 7 : Nouns

## OBJECTIVES

To enable the pupils to know that —

- nouns are words that name things. They name persons, places, animals, objects, actions, states, feelings, qualities and arts/subjects of study.

## FACTS AND RULES

- All the things in the world fall into two classes:
  (*a*) The things that have bodies and can be touched.
  These things include persons, animals, places and objects.
  (*b*) The things that have no bodies and cannot be touched. They can be only felt or thought of.
  These things include actions, states, feelings, qualities and subjects/arts.

## WHAT ARE NOUNS?

*Study the following sentences:*

**A.** 1. **Peter** is very clever.
2. This **cow** is very gentle.
3. A **rose** smells sweet.
4. A **knife** is used to cut with.

**B.** 5. He had a sound **sleep**.
6. **Fatness** makes you ugly.
7. **Poverty** makes us sad.
8. Who does not like **music**?

The words in bold type are names used for things that have no bodies.

*We see that—*

1. **Peter** is the name of a *person.*
2. **Cow** is the name of an *animal* .
3. **Rose** is the name of an *object.*
4. **Knife** is the name of a *thing.*
5. **Sleep** is the name of an *action.*
6. **Fatness** is the name of a *quality.*
7. **Poverty** is the name of a state.
8. **Music** is the name of an art.

All the words in bold type in sentences under **A** and **B** are naming words. Such words are called **nouns**. Remember that the word—**noun**—means *name.*

**A noun is a word that names something.**

# Practice Exercises

## CLASSWORK

I. *Name*:

(a) four persons:

...................... ...................... ...................... ......................

(b) four places:

...................... ...................... ...................... ......................

(c) two animals and two birds:

...................... ...................... ...................... ......................

(d) four things:

...................... ...................... ...................... ......................

(e) four actions:

...................... ...................... ...................... ......................

(f) four qualities:

...................... ...................... ...................... ......................

(g) four feelings:

...................... ...................... ...................... ......................

(h) four states:

...................... ...................... ...................... ......................

(i) two arts and two subjects:

...................... ...................... ...................... ......................

II. *Pick out* **nouns** *and write them in the blanks:*

1. We use a pen to write with. ..................................
2. We had a long race. ..................................
3. The bell is ringing. ..................................
4. The lion is roaring aloud. ..................................
5. Bess and Kate came late. ..................................
6. Beauty cannot be made. ..................................
7. Hunger makes us weak. ..................................

III. *Write a suitable* **noun** *in each blank:*

1. London is a big..........................................................................................
2. A cat is a common......................................................................................
3. ...................................................................................................is a pretty girl.
4. ...............................................................................................is my motherland.
5. ......................................................and.................................went up the hill.
6. Parents love their.......................................................................................
7. A cow has two..........................................................................on its head.
8. Clothes are made of .........................................or...........................................
9. The...................................................................is the king of the forest.
10. The eagle is the king of ..........................................................................
11. Hens and ducks lay..................................................................for us.
12. I have.................................and........................................for breakfast.

IV. *Use each of these* **nouns** *in a sentence:*

1. mother :.......................................................................................
2. teacher :.......................................................................................
3. dog :.......................................................................................
4. Japan :.......................................................................................
5. tea :.......................................................................................
6. cleanliness :.......................................................................................
7. gait :.......................................................................................
8. happiness :.......................................................................................
9. poverty :.......................................................................................
10. painting :.......................................................................................

**Tips For You** Pronounce the word '*cleanliness*' as 'clenliness' not '**cleenliness**'.

## HOMEWORK

V. *Write:*

(a) four nouns naming things in your room:

........................ ........................ ........................ ........................

(b) four nouns naming persons in your family:

........................ ........................ ........................ ........................

(c) four nouns naming vehicles on the road:

........................ ........................ ........................ ........................

(d) four nouns beginning with letter 't':

........................ ........................ ........................ ........................

(e) four nouns ending in letters 'll':

........................ ........................ ........................ ........................

(f) four nouns naming parts of the body:

........................ ........................ ........................ ........................

VI. *What is a* **noun***?*

..........................................................................................................................................

VII. *Use these* **nouns** *in sentences:*

1. gate :..........................................................................................................
2. river :..........................................................................................................
3. weakness :..........................................................................................................
4. school :..........................................................................................................
5. English :..........................................................................................................

VIII. *Write all the different* **nouns** *used in this passage in the blanks given below it:*

A crow was very thirsty. It wanted to drink water. It flew to a garden. There was a small jug under a tree. It had a little water in it. The water was too low for the crow. So the crow put some pebbles into the jug. The water rose up. The crow drank it and flew away.

.................................. .................................. ..................................

.................................. .................................. ..................................

(*6 different nouns*)

# Lesson 8 : Pronouns

## OBJECTIVES

To enable the pupils to know that —

- the word—pronoun = pro + noun = supporter of a noun.
- pronouns are used in place of nouns to avoid their repetition.
- repeating a noun again and again does not sound well. It makes boring English.

## FACTS AND RULES

- Chief pronouns are: I, we, you, he, she, it and they.
- I, we are used by speakers for themselves.
- You is used for the hearer/hearers.
- He is used for a male person other than I, we and you.
- She is used for a female person other than I, we and you.
- It is used for a thing and sometimes for a baby or an animal.
- They is used for more-than-one males, females other than we, you and for things.

## WHAT ARE PRONOUNS?

*Observe these sentences:*

**Tom** is a good boy.

**Tom** is ten years old.

I like **Tom** very much.

**Tom** is very hardworking.

Each of these sentences is about **Tom**. So his name has been repeated. But it sounds funny and boring.

*Now study these sentences:*

*Tom* is a good boy.

**He** is ten years old.

I like **him** very much.

**He** is very hardworking.

These sentences are also about *Tom*. But they sound better. Can you tell, why? Because in them, the words—**He, him, He**—have been used in place of *Tom* which is a noun. These words are **pronouns**. The word—**pronoun**—means the *supporter of a noun*.

**A pronoun is a word used in place of a noun to avoid its repetition.**

## CHIEF PRONOUNS

I

We

You

You

He

She

It

They

**I** is used by a **speaker** for himself.
**We** is used **when the speakers are more than one**.
**You** is used for **a hearer/hearers** by a speaker/speakers.
**He** is used for a **single boy/man** other than **I** and **you**.
**She** is used for a **single girl/lady** other than **I** and **you**.
**It** is used for **a single object** or **a baby** or sometimes for **an animal**.
**They** is used for **many persons/objects** other than **we** and **you**.

## SOME OTHER PRONOUNS

Some other pronouns are formed from each of the eight chief pronouns:

| Chief Pronoun | Other Formed Pronouns | | |
|---|---|---|---|
| **I** | me | mine | myself |
| **we** | us | ours | ourselves |
| **you** | you | yours | yourself, yourselves |
| **he** | him | his | himself |
| **she** | her | hers | herself |
| **it** | it | ....... | itself |
| **they** | them | theirs | themselves |

### Tips For You

- Five words—**my, our, your, its, their**—look like pronouns but they are never used as pronouns. They are used as determiners. (See on page 60-61)
- Two words—**her, his**—are used both as pronouns and determiners.

# Practice Exercises

## CLASSWORK

I. *Pick out* **pronouns** *and write them in the blanks:*

1. The lark is a merry bird. It loves cool air. ......................................
2. Shakespeare was a poet. People loved him. ......................................
3. The dog is a faithful animal. It is a common pet. ......................................
4. I met a little boy. He was ten years old. ................. , ................
5. Clive killed himself at the age of 47. ......................................
6. You should not hurt anybody. ................. , ................
7. Nancy is tall and fair. She is pretty as well. ......................................
8. We beat them with sticks. ................. , ................
9. John has a bat. I also have mine. ......................................
10. Bess was at Zurich. I went to see her. ................. , ................

II. *Write a suitable* **pronoun** *in each blank:*

1. This pen is yours; that is ......................................................................................
2. She will cook food for all of ...............................................................................
3. Why are you weeping? Who has beaten ......................................................?
4. ..............................................................................must always speak the truth.
5. Some men are honest. .......................................................never tell lies.
6. Open this box. .................................................... contains several ornaments.
7. You, ............................................................................................and I are friends.
8. Take your book; I shall take ..............................................................................
9. This frock is mine but that is ..............................................................................
10. These bats are ours but those bats are ......................................................

III. *Use these* **pronouns** *in sentences:*

1. I : ..............................
2. you : ..............................
3. we : ..............................
4. he : ..............................
5. him : ..............................
6. she : ..............................
7. it : ..............................
8. they : ..............................
9. me : ..............................
10. us : ..............................
11. her : ..............................

IV. *Rewrite each sentence replacing the word/words in italics by a* **pronoun***:*

*Example*: This is *my* satchel.

This satchel is **mine**.

1. This is *our* house. ..............................
2. That is not *your* writing. ..............................
3. Which is *her* pen? ..............................
4. Is this *your* school? ..............................
5. These are *my* books. ..............................
6. Are those *your* playthings? ..............................
7. Are these *our* benches? ..............................
8. This is *your* satchel. ..............................
9. These are *her* dolls. ..............................
10. Those are *their* ribbons. ..............................

## HOMEWORK

V. *Use these* **pronouns** *in sentences:*

1. mine : ..............................................................................................
2. yours : ..............................................................................................
3. hers : ..............................................................................................
4. his : ..............................................................................................
5. theirs : ..............................................................................................
6. ours : ..............................................................................................

VI. *What is a* **pronoun***?*

..............................................................................................

..............................................................................................

VII. (a) *Which* **five words** *look like pronouns but are not pronouns? What are they?*

.................. .................. .................. .................. ..................

(b) *Which* **two words** *are used both as pronouns and determiners?*

.................................................... ....................................................

VIII. *Read the passage and sort out different* **pronouns** *used in it. Write them in the blanks provided below:*

A new student has come to our class. He is very untidy. His clothes are dirty and hair unkempt. Perhaps he seldom washes himself. It is very bad. He did not speak to any of us. Ours is a tidy class. The newcomer must mend himself. All my classmates laugh at him. They often put him to shame.

...................... ...................... ...................... ......................

...................... ...................... ...................... *(7 different pronouns)*

IX. *Write the three words in the above paragraph that* **look like pronouns** *but are not pronouns.*

.................................... .................................... ....................................

# Lesson 9 : The Number

## OBJECTIVES

To enable the pupils to know —

- about countable and uncountable nouns.
- the ideas of being one (singular) and many (plural).
- about singular nouns/pronouns and their plural forms.

## FACTS AND RULES

- Most nouns refer to persons, places, animals and objects that have bodies and can be touched.
- These nouns can be counted and each of them can be *only one* or *many* (more than one) in **number**, as:

| | | | |
|---|---|---|---|
| a **chair** | many **chairs** | a **baby** | two **babies** |
| a **house** | several **houses** | a **hare** | three **hares** |

- The noun or pronoun that stands for only one person, place, animal or thing is of **singular number**, as:

  boy cow field table I you he she it

- The noun or pronoun that stands for many (more-than-one) persons, places, animals or things is of **plural number**, as:

  boys cows fields tables we you they

- Remember that **you** is used for not only one person, but also for more-than-one persons.
- **They** is the word used as plural of each of **he**, **she** and **it**.
- Uncountable nouns name things that cannot be counted but only measured, as:

  water sugar milk wheat rice

## COUNTABLES AND UNCOUNTABLES

Most nouns and pronouns refer to persons, animals, places and things. All of them can be counted. So we call them **countable nouns** or simply **countables**.

The nouns that cannot be counted are called **uncountable nouns** or simply **uncountables**. These nouns can only be **measured**.

The following sets of pictures show countable and uncountable nouns:

*Countable Nouns*

*Uncountable Nouns*

## SINGULARS AND PLURALS

Needless to say, a countable noun can be only one or many (more-than-one) in number. So countable nouns fall into two classes:

1. A countable noun is of **singular number**, if it refers to **only one** person, animal, place or thing, as :
   boy, lion, house, chair.
2. A countable noun is of **plural number**, if it refers to many **(more-than-one)** persons, animals, places or things, as:
   boys, lions, houses, chairs.

## FORMING PLURALS

A. *By adding* **s**:

| Singular | Plural | Singular | Plural | Singular | Plural |
|---|---|---|---|---|---|
| ant | ants | fin | fins | inn | inns |
| boy | boys | goat | goats | jar | jars |
| cat | cats | gill | gills | kite | kites |
| dog | dogs | hen | hens | lamp | lamps |
| egg | eggs | desk | desks | mat | mats |
| nib | nibs | owl | owls | pot | pots |
| rat | rats | star | stars | top | tops |
| urn | urns | vest | vests | wall | walls |
| yak | yaks | year | years | zebra | zebras |

B. *By adding* **es** *if the singulars end in* **s, ss, x, ch, sh**:

| Singular | Plural | Singular | Plural | Singular | Plural |
|---|---|---|---|---|---|
| bus | buses | bush | bushes | match | matches |
| box | boxes | watch | watches | brush | brushes |
| class | classes | bench | benches | latch | latches |

C. *By changing* **y** *into* **ies** *if the singulars end in* **y** *after a consonant:*

| Singular | Plural | Singular | Plural | Singular | Plural |
|---|---|---|---|---|---|
| cry | cries | pantry | pantries | story | stories |
| fly | flies | fairy | fairies | sentry | sentries |
| baby | babies | body | bodies | family | families |
| city | cities | sky | skies | country | countries |

D. By adding **s** to singulars if they end in **y** after a vowel:

| Singular | Plural | Singular | Plural | Singular | Plural |
|---|---|---|---|---|---|
| bay | bays | tray | trays | guy | guys |
| day | days | way | ways | monkey | monkeys |
| boy | boys | key | keys | storey | storeys |
| ray | rays | alley | alleys | donkey | donkeys |

E. *By adding* **es** *to singulars ending in* **o** *after a consonant:*

| Singular | Plural | Singular | Plural | Singular | Plural |
|---|---|---|---|---|---|
| hero | heroes | buffalo | buffaloes | mosquito | mosquitoes |
| tomato | tomatoes | negro | negroes | mango | mangoes |
| banjo | banjoes | echo | echoes | potato | potatoes |

*But some singulars ending in* **o** *preceded by a vowel or a consonant form their plurals by just adding the letter* **s** :

| | | | | | |
|---|---|---|---|---|---|
| piano | pianos | cuckoo | cuckoos | bamboo | bamboos |
| radio | radios | solo | solos | photo | photos |

F. *By changing* **f** *or* **fe** *into* **ves**:

| Singular | Plural | Singular | Plural | Singular | Plural |
|---|---|---|---|---|---|
| life | lives | wife | wives | wolf | wolves |
| knife | knives | leaf | leaves | loaf | loaves |

*But for some singulars ending in* **f,** *we just add* **s** :

| | | | | | |
|---|---|---|---|---|---|
| roof | roofs | hoof | hoofs | cliff | cliffs |
| proof | proofs | chief | chiefs | dwarf | dwarfs |

G. *Irregular plurals*:

| Singular | Plural | Singular | Plural | Singular | Plural |
|---|---|---|---|---|---|
| man | men | foot | feet | mouse | mice |
| woman | women | tooth | teeth | dormouse | dormice |
| postman | postmen | goose | geese | louse | lice |
| ox | oxen | child | children | person | people |

H. *Figures, letters and symbols form their plurals by adding* **s** *after an apostrophe:*

| Singular | Plural | Singular | Plural | Singular | Plural |
|---|---|---|---|---|---|
| 5 | 5's | i | i's | B.A. | B.A.'s |
| t | t's | f | f's | 0 | 0's |

I. *Some words have the* **same form** *as singulars and plurals* :

| Singular | Plural | Singular | Plural | Singular | Plural |
|---|---|---|---|---|---|
| sheep | sheep | deer | deer | fish | fish |
| swine | swine | cannon | cannon | fruit | fruit |

J. *Plurals of* **Pronouns**:

| | | | |
|---|---|---|---|
| I → we | me → us | mine → ours | myself → ourselves |
| you → you | you → you | yours → yours | yourself → yourselves |
| he → they | him → them | his → theirs | himself → themselves |
| she → they | her → them | hers → theirs | herself → themselves |
| it → they | it → them | —— → —— | itself → themselves |

K. *Plurals of* **Determiners**:

| | | |
|---|---|---|
| my → our | your → your | his → their |
| her → their | its → their | one's → ones' |
| this → these | that → those | other's → others' |

### Tips For You

- Its is never used as a pronoun but only as a determiner.
- In the past, thou was used for singular you.
- Thy was used for singular your.
- Thine was used for singular yours.
- Thyself was used for yourself.
- All these past words can be seen in poetry even today.

## Practice Exercises

### CLASSWORK

I. *Define:*

(*a*) a countable noun:

..........................................................................................

..........................................................................................

(*b*) an uncountable noun:

..........................................................................................

..........................................................................................

(*c*) a singular noun:

..........................................................................................

..........................................................................................

(*d*) a plural noun:

..........................................................................................

..........................................................................................

II. *Write the* **plural form** *of each of the following*:

| | | | |
|---|---|---|---|
| 1. bamboo | ..................................... | 2. hoof | ..................................... |
| 3. louse | ..................................... | 4. man | ..................................... |
| 5. house | ..................................... | 6. fish | ..................................... |
| 7. sheep | ..................................... | 8. mosquito | ..................................... |
| 9. leaf | ..................................... | 10. tooth | ..................................... |
| 11. you | ..................................... | 12. that | ..................................... |

III. *Write the* **singular form** *of each of the following:*

| | | | |
|---|---|---|---|
| 1. children | ..................................... | 2. people | ..................................... |
| 3. t's | ..................................... | 4. trout | ..................................... |
| 5. tomatoes | ..................................... | 6. oxen | ..................................... |
| 7. fairies | ..................................... | 8. boxes | ..................................... |
| 9. trays | ..................................... | 10. f's | ..................................... |
| 11. them | ..................................... | 12. we | ..................................... |
| 13. our | ..................................... | 14. ours | ..................................... |

IV. *Change the* **number**:

| | | | |
|---|---|---|---|
| 1. 5 | ..................................... | 2. trolley | ..................................... |
| 3. geese | ..................................... | 4. themselves | .......... , .......... , .......... |
| 5. proof | ..................................... | 6. wives | ..................................... |
| 7. women | ..................................... | 8. halo | ..................................... |
| 9. me | ..................................... | 10. this | ..................................... |
| 11. theirs | ..................................... | 12. hers | ..................................... |
| 13. B.A.'s | ..................................... | 14. one's | ..................................... |

## HOMEWORK

IV. *Rewrite each sentence changing* **each singular noun** *to* **plural form**. *Make other necessary changes also.*

1. A piano is very costly.

   ..................................................................................................................

2. This is my book and that is yours.

   ..................................................................................................................

3. A child is generally careless.

   ..................................................................................................................

4. This knife will not cut even a potato.

   ..................................................................................................................

5. A deer is different from a sheep.

   ..................................................................................................................

V. *Rewrite each sentence changing* **each plural noun** *to* **singular form**. *Make other necessary changes also.*

1. We are human beings.

   ..................................................................................................................

2. Cows give us milk.

   ..................................................................................................................

3. Mothers love their babies.

   ..................................................................................................................

4. Negroes live in Africa.

   ..................................................................................................................

5. Geese can swim but hens cannot.

   ..................................................................................................................

6. My teeth are aching.

   ..................................................................................................................

7. The mice wanted to get rid of the cats.

   ..................................................................................................................

# Lesson 10 : The Gender

## OBJECTIVES

To enable the pupils to know —

- the meaning of the word—gender.
- the ideas of being a male and a female.
- the meanings of common gender and neuter gender.
- about four types of gender.

## FACTS AND RULES

- Gender refers to sex, i.e. whether a noun/pronoun refers to a male or a female.
- A noun/pronoun referring to a male is of masculine gender, as:

  boy bull king lion husband father
- A noun/pronoun referring to a female is of feminine gender, as:

  girl cow queen lioness wife mother
- A noun/pronoun referring to someone that can be a male or a female is of common gender, as:

  baby student teacher doctor friend speaker
- A noun/pronoun referring to a lifeless object (that is neither a male nor a female) is of neuter gender, as:

  stool bed book shirt pencil purse
- Natural objects known for their strength/greatness are of masculine gender, as:

  sun storm war blood summer death
- Natural objects known for their beauty and grace are of feminine gender, as:

  moon earth Nature spring motherland

## GENDER

*Gender* means *sex*. Living things fall into two classes with respect to sex. They are either **males** or **females**.

But there are living things about whom it cannot be said whether they are male or female. They are common to both the sexes. Such things are of **common gender**.

Non-living things do not come under any sex. So all lifeless things are of **neuter gender**.

## FOUR TYPES OF GENDER

There are four genders:

1. **Masculine Gender : Males**

man

dog

king

monk

2. **Feminine Gender : Females**

woman

bitch

queen

nun

3. **Common Gender : Used for both Sexes**

child

teacher

friend

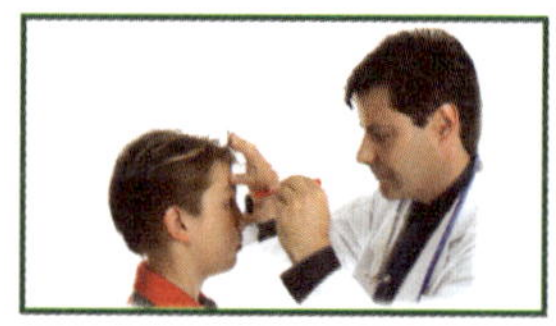
doctor

4. **Neuter Gender : Sexless Objects**

table

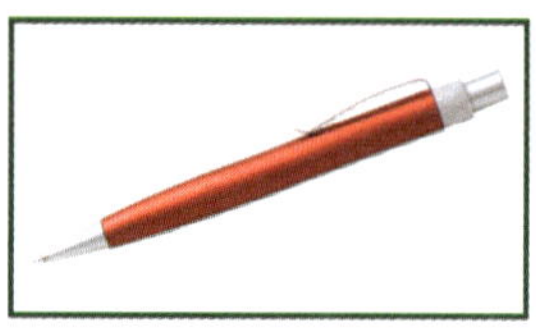
pen

desk

wall

## FORMING FEMININES

### A. Irregular Feminines:

| *Masculine* | *Feminine* | *Masculine* | *Feminine* |
|---|---|---|---|
| boy | girl | king | queen |
| father | mother | master | mistress |
| son | daughter | hero | heroine |
| man | woman | brother | sister |
| lad | lass | widower | widow |
| bridegroom | bride | emperor | empress |
| he | she | his | her |

| *Masculine* | *Feminine* | *Masculine* | *Feminine* |
|---|---|---|---|
| bachelor | maid | sir | madam |
| cock | hen | buck/stag | doe (deer) |
| stallion | mare | wizard | witch |
| colt | filly | nephew | niece |
| drake | duck | horse | mare |
| drone | queen (bee) | ram | ewe |
| gander | goose | dog fox | vixen |
| uncle | aunt | mr | miss |
| bull | cow | landlord | landlady |
| billy | nanny (goat) | milkman | milkmaid |
| cock | hen | monk | nun |
| bull-elephant | cow-elephant | peacock | peahen |
| manservant | maidservant | tomcat | queen |

B. **By adding *ess*:**

| *Masculine* | *Feminine* | *Masculine* | *Feminine* |
|---|---|---|---|
| actor | actress | duke | duchess |
| emperor | empress | tiger | tigress |
| waiter | waitress | negro | negress |
| lion | lioness | prince | princess |
| god | goddess | giant | giantess |

C. **Words of common gender**:

| | | | | |
|---|---|---|---|---|
| baby | child | cousin | enemy | friend |
| monarch | student | bird | neighbour | parent |
| thief | orphan | person | pupil | teacher |
| singer | cook | officer | manager | speaker |
| author | heir | actor | waiter | host |

D. **Words of neuter gender**:

| chair | table | pen | pencil | stool |
|---|---|---|---|---|
| cot | book | tree | room | desk |

E. **Objects known for strength or greatness are of masculine gender:**

Sun Death Summer Time Famine War Storm Flood

F. **Objects known for their grace and beauty are of feminine gender:**

Moon Earth Spring Nature Providence

G. **Nouns of quality are of feminine gender:**

love mercy charity hope justice truth patience

## Tips For You

The words—ship and train—are treated as feminines, as:

1. The ship cast **her** anchor at last.
2. The train caught **her** speed in a few minutes.

The words—sun and death—are treated as **masculines**, as:

1. The sun was so bright and harsh that we needed sunglasses to face **him**.
2. Death is cruel and **he** spares none.

# Practice Exercises

## CLASSWORK

I. *Define:*

(*a*) masculine gender:

.......................................................................................................

(*b*) feminine gender:

.......................................................................................................

(*c*) common gender:

.......................................................................................................

(*d*) neuter gender:

.......................................................................................................

II. *Write the names of:*

(*a*) four *genders*:

.......................... .......................... .......................... ..........................

(*b*) four natural objects that are *masculines*:

.......................... .......................... .......................... ..........................

(*c*) four natural objects that are *feminines*:

.......................... .......................... .......................... ..........................

(*d*) four nouns of *common gender*:

.......................... .......................... .......................... ..........................

(*e*) four nouns of *neuter gender*:

.......................... .......................... .......................... ..........................

(*f*) two vehicles treated as *feminines*:

.......................... .......................... .......................... ..........................

(*g*) two lands treated as *feminines*:

.......................... .......................... .......................... ..........................

III. *Write the* **feminines** *of the following*:

| | | | |
|---|---|---|---|
| 1. uncle | .......................... | 2. lion | .......................... |
| 3. nephew | .......................... | 4. drake | .......................... |
| 5. buck | .......................... | 6. monk | .......................... |
| 7. peacock | .......................... | 8. gander | .......................... |
| 9. giant | .......................... | 10. boy | .......................... |
| 11. lad | .......................... | 12. master | .......................... |
| 13. cock | .......................... | 14. son | .......................... |
| 15. bull | .......................... | 16. fox | .......................... |
| 17. ram | .......................... | 18. stag | .......................... |
| 19. colt | .......................... | 20. drone | .......................... |

IV. *Write the* **masculines** *of the following*:

| | | | | | |
|---|---|---|---|---|---|
| 1. | wife | ............................ | 2. | daughter | ............................ |
| 3. | widow | ............................ | 4. | bride | ............................ |
| 5. | lady | ............................ | 6. | filly | ............................ |
| 7. | ewe | ............................ | 8. | nun | ............................ |
| 9. | queen | ............................ | 10. | goose | ............................ |
| 11. | she-goat | ............................ | 12. | milkmaid | ............................ |

## HOMEWORK

V. *Change the* **gender**:

| | | | | | |
|---|---|---|---|---|---|
| 1. | heroine | ............................ | 2. | emperor | ............................ |
| 3. | miss | ............................ | 4. | bride | ............................ |
| 5. | drone | ............................ | 7. | father | ............................ |
| 9. | doe | ............................ | 10. | goose | ............................ |
| 1l . | boar | ............................ | 12. | cow | ............................ |

VI. *Rewrite these sentences changing the gender of nouns from* **masculine** *to* **feminine**:

1. The tiger sprang at the bull.

   ................................................................................................................

2. His uncle sent him a present.

   ................................................................................................................

3. We saw stags, bucks and peacocks at the zoo.

   ................................................................................................................

4. The bridegroom is a handsome lad.

   ................................................................................................................

5. The headmaster is on leave today.

   ................................................................................................................

6. The landlord rebuked his manservant.

.....................................................................................................

7. Boys can't be men and bulls can't be horses.

.....................................................................................................

VII. *Rewrite these sentences changing the gender from* **feminine** *to* **masculine**:

1. The princess paid a visit to her mother.

.....................................................................................................

2. The lioness is lying under a shady tree.

.....................................................................................................

3. Nuns are women of great piety.

.....................................................................................................

4. May I come in, madam?

.....................................................................................................

5. The milkmaid met a witch on the way.

.....................................................................................................

6. The empress called the princess to her chamber.

.....................................................................................................

7. Her mistress is a very kind woman.

.....................................................................................................

VIII. *Fill in each blank with the* **correct word** *from within brackets*:

1. Nature is at..................................................best in March. (*his, her*)
2. The light of the sun travels through..................................rays. (*his, her*)
3. Love has......................................................own charms. (*his, her*)
4. A good child loves..................................................parents. (*his, her, its*)
5. The baby is crying. ..................................................is hungry. (*It. He, She*)
6. India is our motherland. We love ......................... very much. (*him, her*)

# Lesson 11 : The Person

## OBJECTIVES

To enable the pupils to know that —

- a person who speaks to another person is the first person.
- the person whom the first person speaks to is the second person.
- any noun/pronoun other than the first person and the second person is the third person.
- the words I, we, me, us, my, mine, our, ours, myself and ourselves are pronouns of the first person.
- the words you, yours, yourself and yourselves are pronouns of the second person.
- the words he, she, it him, his, her, its, hers, they, them, their, theirs, himself, herself, itself and themselves are pronouns of the third person.
- All naming words (nouns) are words of the third person.

## FACTS AND RULES

- There are three persons in all in English.
- The person who speaks *i.e.,* the speaker.
- The person who is spoken to *i.e.,* the hearer.
- The person other than these two persons about whom they both talk.
- Each person has its words of singular and plural number.

| Person | Singular Words | Plural Words |
|---|---|---|
| First Person | I, me, my, mine, myself | we, us, our, ours, ourselves |
| Second Person | you, your, yours, yourself | you, your, yours, yourselves |
| Third Person | he, him, his, himself<br>she, her, hers, herself<br>it, its, itself | they, them, their, theirs,<br>themselves |

## THREE PERSONS

The pronouns **I, we, you, he, she, it** and **they** fall into three classes of persons — first person, second person and third person — as shown below.

### FIRST PERSON PRONOUNS

I am a boy,

We are students.

### SECOND PERSON PRONOUNS

You are a girl.

You are girls.

### THIRD PERSON PRONOUNS

He is a player.

She is a woman.

It is a ball.

They are nurses.

1. The pronoun I stands for the person who speaks.
2. The pronoun we stands for two or more persons speaking together.

I and we are pronouns of the first person

3. The word you stands for the person spoken to.
4. The word you also stands for two or more persons spoken to together.

You (singular) and You (plural) are pronouns of the second person

5. The word he stands for a male other than the speaker and the hearer.
6. The word she stands for a female other the speaker and the hearer.
7. The word it stands for a lifeless object talked about by the speaker and the hearer.
8. The word they stands for the persons other than the speaker and the hearer.

He, she, it and they are pronouns of the third person

So, there are three persons in all:

1. The person who speaks (*speaker*).
2. The person who is spoken to (*hearer*).
3. The person other than these two persons *i.e.* the person *about whom the above two persons talk.*

## FIRST PERSON

**The person who speaks is called the first person.**

The words — *I, we, me, us, my, our, mine, ours, myself, ourselves* — are words of the **first person**.

*I, me, my, mine, myself* are words of the **first person in singular number**.

*We, us, our, ours, ourselves* are words of the **first person in plural number**.

## SECOND PERSON

**The person who is spoken to is called the second person.**

The words — *you, your, yours, yourself, yourselves* — are words of the **second person.**

*You, your, yours, yourself* are words of the **second person** in **singular number.**

*You, your, yours, yourselves* are words of the **second person** in **plural number.**

## THIRD PERSON

**The person/persons other than the speaker and the hearer and about whom they talk is called the third person.**

*He, she, it, him, her, his, hers, its, their, theirs, himself, herself, itself, themselves* are words of the ***third person***.

*He, him, his, himself, she, her, herself, hers, it, its, itself* are words of the **third person in singular number**.

*They, them, their, theirs, themselves* are words of the **third person in plural number**.

## Tips For You

- The second person **'you'** refers to **both singular and plural numbers.**
- Any singular **noun** about whom something is said, is of the third person singular number, as: *John, chair, village, book, etc.*
- It is very important to understand what third person singular number is because it mostly needs a special verb for itself.

# Practice Exercises

## CLASSWORK

I. *Sort out* **words of the first person** *and write them in the blanks*:

1. Jenny gave me a new pen. ..............................................
2. Daddy bought me a hat. ..............................................
3. Our teachers are very able. ..............................................
4. We ourselves shall do it. ..............................................
5. My school has a big building. ..............................................
6. I myself have done this job. ....................,..........................
7. The teacher taught us a new lesson. ..............................................
8. We cannot do it by ourselves. ....................,..........................

II. *Sort out* **words of the second person** *and write them in the blanks:*

1. You are my best friend. ..............................................
2. I shall help you in every way. ..............................................
3. Where is your father? ..............................................
4. You yourself can go there. ....................,..........................
5. That watch is yours. ..............................................
6. You must behave yourself. ....................,..........................

III. *Sort out* **words of the third person** *and write them in the blanks:*

1. He is in class VII. ..........................................
2. She is tall and slim. ..........................................
3. They helped us in trouble. ..........................................
4. It is your pencil. ..........................................
5. They are labourers. ..........................................
6. We met them at the fair. ..........................................
7. They themselves are to blame for it. ..........................................

IV. *Name —*

1. the person who speaks : ..........................................
2. the person who is spoken to : ..........................................
3. the person other than the speaker and the hearer : ..........................................

## HOMEWORK

V. *Write the* **person** *and the* **number** *of each word in italics:*

| | Person | Number |
|---|---|---|
| 1. *He* is a gentle lad. | .......................... | .......................... |
| 2. *We* must speak the truth. | .......................... | .......................... |
| 3. *You* are very hardworking. | .......................... | .......................... |
| 4. *She* is tall and slim. | .......................... | .......................... |
| 5. *They* are all thieves. | .......................... | .......................... |
| 6. *It* is a grand house. | .......................... | .......................... |
| 7. *I* am not a saint. | .......................... | .......................... |
| 8. *You* are all very good players. | .......................... | .......................... |

VI. *What is meant by the* **first person**? *Give two examples:*

..............................................................................................................................

..............................................................................................................................

*Examples* 1. ..........................................................................................................

2. ..........................................................................................................

VII. *What is meant by the* **second person**? *Give two examples:*

..............................................................................................................................

..............................................................................................................................

*Examples* 1. ..........................................................................................................

2. ..........................................................................................................

VIII. *What is meant by the* **third person**? *Give two examples:*

..............................................................................................................................

..............................................................................................................................

*Examples* 1. ..........................................................................................................

2. ..........................................................................................................

IX. *What is meant by the* **third person singular number**? *Why is it important to understand it clearly? Give two examples:*

..............................................................................................................................

..............................................................................................................................

..............................................................................................................................

..............................................................................................................................

*Examples* 1. ..........................................................................................................

2. ..........................................................................................................

# Lesson 12 : Determiners : A, An, The

## OBJECTIVES

To enable the pupils to know that —

- a word that points to a noun definitely or indefinitely is called a determiner.
- the words — a, an — refer to nouns indefinitely. In other words, either of them points to any noun of a class, not a particular one.
- the word — the — refers to a noun definitely, *i.e.* it points to a particular noun.

## FACTS AND RULES

- We use a/an before a noun when it is used for the first time, as:
  1. Once there was a *farmer*. .......(any farmer)
  2. An ant was carrying a grain of rice. ........(any ant)
- We use the before a noun when it is repeated, as:
  1. Once there was a *farmer*. The farmer was very old. .......(same farmer)
  2. An ant was carrying a grain of rice. The ant was hardworking. ........(same ant)
- We use a before a singular noun that starts with a consonant sound, as:

  a book  a pen  a fruit-seller  a skier  a bench
- We use an before a singular noun that starts with a vowel sound, as:

  an ant  an elephant  an ink-pot  an hour  an American
- The is used before the names of some natural objects, as :

  the sun  the moon  the sky  the earth
- The is used before the names of rivers, mountains, books, communities, as:

  the Thames  the Bible  the Himalayas  the English

## DETERMINERS

*Observe these sentences:*

1. I bought **a** book yesterday.
2. He eats **an** egg daily.
3. **The** Himalayas are the highest mountains.

*We see that —*

1. ***a*** refers to the noun *book* which means *any book.*
2. ***an*** refers to the noun *egg* which means *any egg.*
3. ***the*** refers to a *particular mountain* — Himalayas.

**A, an, the** are just small words used before nouns to determine them definitely or indefinitely. So they are called **determiners**.

Determiners **are small words that determine nouns definitely or indefinitely.**

## USE OF A, AN

1. **A, an** are used before singular countable nouns that are not proper nouns.
2. **A** is used before singular countable nouns beginning with consonant sounds, as:

   *a* book    *a* jug    *a* European    *a* king    *a* tub

3. **An** is used before singular countable nouns beginning with vowel sounds, as:

   *an* ant    *an* egg    *an* urn    *an* ox    *an* ink-pot    *an* eye

## USE OF THE

1. **The** is used before the names of rivers, mountain ranges, oceans, books, nations, etc., as:

   *the* Amazon    *the* Himalayas    *the* Bible    *the* French

2. **The** is used before a common noun that is only one of its kind, as:

   *the* sun    *the* moon    *the* earth    *the* sky

3. When we speak of a noun for the first time, we use **a** or **an** before it. But when we speak of it again, we use **the** before it, as:

   A man lived in *a* village.    The man was very honest.

4. **The** is used before the names of **communities,** as:

   the Muslims,    the Hindus,    the Christians

# Practice Exercises

## CLASSWORK

I. *Write **a** or **an** in each blank:*

| | | | | | |
|---|---|---|---|---|---|
| 1. | .........elephant | 2. | .........bat | 3. | .........leg |
| 4. | .........ink-pot | 5. | .........owl | 6. | .........buffalo |
| 7. | .........mouse | 8. | .........apple | 9. | .........teacher |
| 10. | .........traveller | 11. | .........inn | 12. | .........horse |

II. *Fill in each blank with **a** or **an**:*

1. This is.......................................................................................ripe apple.
2. I heard.......................................................................................loud noise.
3. He bought..................................................................................ice-cream.
4. Iron is.......................................................................................useful metal.
5. We have formed.........................................................................union.
6. ...........................................................honest man is respected everywhere.
7. This hen lays.............................................................egg every day.

III. *Tick (✓) the correct use of **a**, **an** and cross (×) the incorrect one:*

| | | | | | |
|---|---|---|---|---|---|
| 1. | a egg | ( ) | 2. | a basket | ( ) |
| 3. | an orange | ( ) | 4. | a urinal | ( ) |
| 5. | a dream | ( ) | 6. | an hour | ( ) |
| 7. | a friend | ( ) | 8. | an pupil | ( ) |
| 9. | a M.A | ( ) | 10. | an B.A. | ( ) |

IV. *Write **a, an** or **the** in each blank:*

| | | | | | |
|---|---|---|---|---|---|
| 1. | .........Nile | 2. | .........town | 3. | .........urn |
| 4. | .........owl | 5. | .........hospital | 6. | .........apple |
| 7. | .........Christians | 8. | .........Bible | 9. | .........heir |

V. *Fill up each blank with* **a, an** *or* **the** *:*

1. He is as stupid as..................................................................................donkey.
2. The farmer bought....................cow,..................ox and.....................mare.
3 ..........................Bible and........................Bhagwad Gita are sacred books.
4 ...........................................Himalayas are higher than any other mountain.
5 ..............................................................................................sky is all about us.

## HOMEWORK

VI. *Write* **a** *or* **an** or **the** *in each blank :*

| | | | |
|---|---|---|---|
| 1. | ..........................useful metal | 2. | .......................................old man |
| 3. | .......................easy language | 4. | ...............................tough question |
| 5. | .........................new umbrella | 6. | ........................................untidy girl |
| 7. | ..................................British | 8. | ..................moon and............sun |
| 9. | .........................................island in | | .......................................Pacific Ocean |
| 10. | ..................................French and | | ...............................................English |

VII. *Fill up each blank with* **a** *or* **an** *or* **the** *:*

1. English is the language of..................................................................English.
2. Sri Lanka is....................................island in..........................Indian Ocean.
3. .........................................sun shines by day and..................moon at night.
4. My father gave me.................orange and.......................................mango.
5. Your clock is........................................................................................hour too fast.

VIII. *Insert* **a**, **an** *or* **the** *as is suitable in each blank:*

Once........................................farmer lived in................................certain village. .....................village had...............inn and..............temple. ..................farmer. was.....................................God-fearing man. He daily went to........................ temple for worship. It was just outside......................................................village.

# Lesson 13 : Possessive Words

## OBJECTIVES

To enable the pupils to know that —

- every personal pronoun has two possessive forms.
- one of these forms is used as a determiner and the other as a pronoun.
- the possessive words—my, our, your, his, her, its, their—are used as determiners.
- the possessive words—mine, ours, yours, his, hers, theirs—are used as pronouns.
- the possessive word—his—is used both as a pronoun and as a determiner.
- the possessive word—its—is always used as a determiner. It is never used as a pronoun.

## FACTS AND RULES

- The possessive words — my, our, your, his, her, its, their — are always followed by nouns, as:

  1. My *name* is Joe.
  2. Our *school* has a big building.
  3. Where is your *book*?
  4. His *father* is a doctor.
  5. Her *mother* is a nurse.
  6. It is a hare. Its *ears* are long.
  7. They are all players. Their *bats* are inside the room.

  In each of the above sentences, the word in red colour points to the noun following it in a definite manner. So each of them is a definite determiner.

- All the words in red colour in the above seven sentences are possessive words. So they are possessive determiners.

- The possessive words — mine, ours, yours, his, hers, theirs — are pronouns. They stand independently for nouns. They are never followed by nouns, as:

  1. This *bat* is mine.
  2. That book is *yours*.
  3. These bags are ours.
  4. That shirt is his.
  5. This ribbon is hers.
  6. Those toys are theirs.

  In each of the above sentences, the word in red colour stands in place of a noun independently. It is not followed by any noun. So it is a possessive pronoun.

- Note the difference between the possessive determiners and possessive pronouns. The possessive determiners are followed by nouns but the possessive pronouns stand alone in place of their nouns.

## POSSESSIVE WORDS

*Observe the table given below:*

| *Personal Pronouns* | *Possessive Pronouns* | *Possessive Determiners* |
|---|---|---|
| I | mine | my |
| We | ours | our |
| You | yours | your |
| He | his | his |
| She | hers | her |
| It | _____ | its |
| They | theirs | their |

## POSSESSIVE DETERMINERS

There are seven possessive determiners — **my, our, your, his, her, its their —** formed from personal pronouns. These determiners are used before nouns. Each of these determiners points to the noun that comes after it in a definite way.

*Observe the following sentences*:

1. My *book* is on the table.
2. We must love our *motherland*.
3. Where have you put your *toy*?
4. His *hair* is black and curly.
5. Her *mother* is looking for her.
6. Here is a table. Its *top* is oval.
7. Their *bags* are on the shelf.

Each sentence has a word printed in red colour. It is a possessive word and has a noun after it. It points to that noun in a definite manner. So it is a **possessive determiner**.

## POSSESSIVE PRONOUNS

Observe the table given on the previous page once again. It shows six possessive pronouns — **mine, ours, yours, his, hers, theirs** — formed from personal pronouns. These possessive pronouns stand for their nouns quite independently, as:

1. This shirt is mine.
2. These toys are not ours.
3. Is this cap yours?
4. This bag is his, not mine.
5. Is that ribbon hers?
6. Are these books theirs?

Each sentence has a word printed in red colour. It is a possessive word and stands for a noun. It shows the possession of that noun over something. So it is a **possessive pronoun.**

### Tips For You

- Possessive words are small words formed from personal pronouns.
- Possessive words fall into two classes – possessive determiners and possessive pronouns.
- A possessive determiner is a small word that shows the possession of a certain noun that follows it.
- A possessive pronoun is a small word that shows the possession of a certain noun by another noun or pronoun for which it itself stands.
- The difference between possessive determiners and possessive pronouns lies in two facts that are given below:
  1. They differ in spelling.
  2. Whereas possessive determiners are followed by their nouns, possessive pronouns stand alone for their nouns.
- The possessive word – his –is both a determiner and a pronoun, as:
  1. This is his *book*. ......(*determiner*)  2. This *book* is his. ......(*pronoun*)

# Practice Exercises

## CLASSWORK

I. (*a*) *Write the seven personal pronouns in the given blanks:*

.......................... .......................... .......................... ..........................

.......................... .......................... ..........................

(*b*) *Write the possessive word formed from each given personal pronoun:*

1. I ........... ...............
2. We ........... ...............
3. You (*sing.*) ........... ...............
4. You (*plu.*) ........... ...............
5. He ........... ...............
6. She ........... ...............
7. It ...........
8. They ........... ...............

II. *Write the possessive determiner formed from each personal pronoun:*

1. I ...............
2. We ............
3. You ............
4. You ............
5. He ...............
6. She ............
7. It ............
8. They ............

III. *Write the possessive pronoun formed from each personal pronoun:*

1. I ...............
2. We ...............
3. You ............
4. He ...............
5. She ...............
6. They ............

IV. *Use each given possessive determiner in a sentence:*

1. My : ..........................................................................................
2. Our : ..........................................................................................
3. Your : ..........................................................................................
4. His : ..........................................................................................
5. Her : ..........................................................................................
6. Its : ..........................................................................................
7. Their : ..........................................................................................

V. *Use each given possessive pronoun in a sentence:*

1. Mine : ..............................................................................................
2. Ours : ..............................................................................................
3. Yours : ..............................................................................................
4. His : ..............................................................................................
5. Hers : ..............................................................................................
6. Theirs : ..............................................................................................

## HOMEWORK

VI. *Sort out the possessive word in each sentence and write whether it is a determiner or a pronoun:*

| *Sentence* | *Word* | *Determiner/ Pronoun* |
|---|---|---|
| 1. Where is your motorcycle? | ................ | ............................... |
| 2. This beautiful pen is mine. | ................ | ............................... |
| 3. This yellow frock is hers. | ................ | ............................... |
| 4. Here are their playthings. | ................ | ............................... |
| 5. This mango-garden is ours. | ................ | ............................... |
| 6. This pet dog is his. Its tail is curly. | ........,........ | ................,.............. |
| 7. Are these dolls theirs? | ................ | ............................... |

VII. *Fill in each blank with a suitable possessive determiner:*

1. ...................... village stands on a hill-side.
2. Where is .................................. red ribbon?
3. Susan likes ...................... doll very much.
4. ........................... elder brother is a doctor.
5. This is ........ pet cat. .............. fur is white.
6. ...................... uniforms are really very fine.

# Lesson 14 : Demonstrative Words

## OBJECTIVES

To enable the pupils to know that —

- there are six demonstrative words used in English.
- these six demonstrative words are — this, that, these, those, same, such.
- these six demonstrative words are used both as determiners and pronouns.
- when used as determiners, these words are followed by their nouns.
- when used as pronouns, these words stand alone for their nouns.

## FACTS AND RULES

- There are six demonstrative words in all — this, that, these, those, same, such.
- These six words either point to their nouns definitely or stand alone for their nouns.
- When these words point to their nouns, they are followed by those nouns, as:
  1. This *book* has interesting stories.
  2. That *frock* looks good on you.
  3. These *players* have come from Delhi.
  4. Those *dolls* are very costly.
  5. We were *looking* in the same direction.
  6. Such people are always respected.
- In each of the above sentences, the word in red colour points definitely to the noun that follows it. So each of them is a demonstrative determiner.
- When these words stand alone for their nouns, they act as pronouns, as:
  1. This is all nonsense.
  2. That is really useful.
  3. Whose books are these?
  4. Those are our bats.
  5. If you will have tea, I will *do* the same.
  6. Such was not my intention.
- In each of the above sentences, the word in red colour stands in place of a noun independently. It is not followed by any noun. So it is a demonstrative pronoun.
- Note the difference between demonstrative determiners and demonstrative pronouns. The demonstrative determiners are followed by nouns and point to them definitely. But the demonstrative pronouns stand alone in place of their nouns.

## DEMONSTRATIVE WORDS

*Observe the pictures and the sentences given below :*

This ball is mine.

[This points to a nearby thing.]

That kite is blue.

[That points to a far-off thing.]

Get me the same toy.

[Same points to just that very thing.]

These balls are mine.

[These points to nearby things.]

Those kites are red.

[Those points to far-off things.]

Such a car is costly.

[Such points to a similar thing.]

## DEMONSTRATIVE DETERMINERS

There are six demonstrative determiners — **this, that, these, those, same, such**. These determiners are used before nouns. Each of them points to the noun that comes after it in a definite manner.

*Observe the following sentences:*

1. I do not like this *shirt* at all.
2. That *house* belongs to my uncle.
3. Put these *mangoes* in a basket.
4. Get those *chairs* polished.
5. Tell me the same *story* again.
6. I like such *toys* very much.

Each sentence has a word printed in red colour. It is a demonstrative word and it has a noun printed in italics after it. It points to that noun definitely. So it is a demonstrative determiner.

## DEMONSTRATIVE PRONOUNS

Observe the pictures given on the previous page once again. The six demonstrative words — **this, that, these, those, same, such** — can be used in another way also. Instead of being used before nouns they can stand for nouns independently, as:

1. Whose *skirt* is this?
2. This *ribbon* is finer than that.
3. How many *bags* are these?
4. Whose *toys* are those?
5. If you go for a *walk*, I will do the same.
6. Welcome a *guest* as such.

Each sentence has a word printed in red colour. It is a demonstrative word and stands for the noun printed in italics. It also points to the noun for which it stands. So it is a **demonstrative pronoun.**

### Tips For You

- Demonstrative words are small words that point to nouns definitely.
- Demonstrative words fall into two classes – demonstrative determiners and demonstrative pronouns.
- A demonstrative determiner is a small word that points to a certain noun that follows it.
- A demonstrative pronoun is a small word that stands for a certain noun and also points to it.
- The difference between demonstrative determiners and demonstrative pronouns lies in the fact that:

  whereas demonstrative determiners are followed by their nouns, demonstrative pronouns stand alone for their nouns.
- Remember that the words this, these refer to nearby things while the words that, those point to far-off things.

# Practice Exercises

## CLASSWORK

I. (*a*) *Write the six demonstrative words in the blanks given below:*

........................................ ........................................ ........................................

........................................ ........................................ ........................................

(*b*) *Write the correct demonstrative word that —*

1. points to a nearby thing. ................
2. points to a far-off thing. ................
3. points to just that very thing. ................
4. points to a thing that is similar or almost alike. ................
5. points to nearby things. ................
6. points to far-off things. ................

II. *Fill in each blank with a suitable word:*

1. A demonstrative word points to a noun ...................................... .
2. A demonstrative determiner is used ............... the noun it points to.
3. A demonstrative pronoun is ................... for a noun that it points to.

III. *Use each of the given words as a demonstrative determiner:*

1. This : ..........................................................................................................
2. Same : ..........................................................................................................
3. Those : ..........................................................................................................
4. That : ..........................................................................................................
5. These : ..........................................................................................................
6. Such : ..........................................................................................................

IV. *Use each of the given words as a demonstrative pronoun:*

1. This : ..........................................................................................

2. Same : ..........................................................................................

3. Those : ..........................................................................................

4. That : ..........................................................................................

5. These : ..........................................................................................

6. Such : ..........................................................................................

## HOMEWORK

V. *Sort out the demonstrative word in each sentence and write whether it is a determiner or a pronoun:*

| Sentence | Word | Determiner/Pronoun |
|---|---|---|
| 1. Whose is that motorcycle? | ................. | .................................. |
| 2. Whose frock is this? | ................. | .................................. |
| 3. My story is exactly the same. | ................. | .................................. |
| 4. I like such playthings very much. | ................. | .................................. |
| 5. Those mangoes are ripe and juicy. | ................. | .................................. |
| 6. Whose shoes are these? | ................. | .................................. |

VI. *Put a suitable word in each blank. Write whether it is a determiner or a pronoun:*

| Sentence | Word | Determiner/Pronoun |
|---|---|---|
| 1. .............. village has 50 houses. | ................. | .................................. |
| 2. Whose ribbon is ....................? | ................. | .................................. |
| 3. A guest must be treated as ........... . | ................. | .................................. |
| 4. ...................... pens are very costly. | ................. | .................................. |
| 5. I will do the ............ if you have milk. | ................. | .................................. |
| 6. Bring all ............... books to me. | ................. | .................................. |

# Lesson 15 : Adjectives

## OBJECTIVES

To enable the pupils to know that —

- the word — adjective — is pronounced ajektiv as it has its d silent.
- an adjective adds to the meaning of a noun. In other words, it states some good or bad quality of its noun.
- an adjective has three forms that are called its degrees.
- adjectives are generally used before their nouns. But they can also be used after the verbs that follow their nouns.

## FACTS AND RULES

- An adjective is a word that stands for a quality of its noun, as:
  1. The parrot is a green *bird*.
  2. Susan is a tall slim *girl*.
  3. That *frock* is very costly.
- Adjectives are generally used before their nouns as in sentences 1 and 2 given above.
- An adjective can also be used after the verb that follows its noun as in sentence 3 given above.
- If two or three adjectives are used for a noun before it, no comma, etc. is put between those adjectives, as:
  1. Kate is a tall slim pretty *girl*.
  2. Robert is a short strong handsome *boy*.
  3. The Himalayas are a high charming snowy *mountain*.
- But if two or three adjectives are used for a noun after the verb of the sentence, commas, etc. are used between them, as:
  1. Kate is very tall, slim and pretty.
  2. Robert is short, strong and handsome.
  3. The Himalayas are very high, charming and snowy.
- Adjectives must not be confused with determiners. Words of number or quantity and interrogative words (what, which, etc.) are not adjectives but determiners.

*Observe these sentences:*

1. The camel is a **tall** animal.
2. The rat is a **small** animal.
3. Here is ice. It is **cold**.
4. Here is tea. It is **hot**.
5. Annie is a **plump fair pretty** girl.
6. Betty has a **white** dress on.
7. A **beautiful** woman sat on a sofa.
8. This book has **interesting** stories in it.
9. This baby is very **fair**, **lovely** and **healthy**.

*We see that—*

1. The word '**tall**' qualifies the noun animal used for *camel*.
2. The word '**small**' qualifies the noun animal used for *rat*.
3. The word '**cold'** qualifies the pronoun it used for *ice*.
4. The word '**hot'** qualifies the pronoun it used for *tea*.
5. The words '**plump, fair, pretty**' qualify the noun girl used for *Annie*.
6. The word '**white**' qualifies the noun *dress*.
7. The word '**beautiful**' describes the noun *woman*.
8. The word '**interesting**' describes the noun *stories*.
9. The words '**fair, lovely** and **healthy**' describe the noun *baby*.

All the words in bold type are **qualifying** words. They qualify nouns or pronouns in red colour. In other words, they add something to the meanings of their nouns/pronouns. So, they are called **adjectives.**

**An adjective is a word that qualifies a noun or a pronoun.**

# Practice Exercises

## CLASSWORK

I. *Sort out the* **adjectives** *and write them in the blanks:*

| | Sentences | Adjectives |
|---|---|---|
| 1. | It was a fine day. | .............................................. |
| 2. | The greedy dog jumped into the water. | .............................................. |
| 3. | His cold hands felt like ice. | .............................................. |
| 4. | The poor man was in rags. | .............................................. |
| 5. | These grapes have a sour taste. | .............................................. |
| 6. | Jane is pretty and slim. | ......................,...................... |
| 7. | Stars look like tiny lamps. | .............................................. |
| 8. | They are fussy children. | .............................................. |
| 9. | The earth is round in shape. | .............................................. |
| 10. | This boy is very rude. | .............................................. |

II. *Use these* **adjectives** *in sentences:*

1. beautiful : ................................................................................................
2. clear : ................................................................................................
3. dull : ................................................................................................
4. easy : ................................................................................................
5. foolish : ................................................................................................
6. greedy : ................................................................................................
7. high : ................................................................................................
8. lazy : ................................................................................................
9. neat : ................................................................................................
10. honest : ................................................................................................

III. *Write a suitable* **adjective** *in each blank:*

(*a*)

1. a ..........................child
2. a.................................woman
3. ........................weather
4. .......................................hair
5. ...........................grass
6. a.......................................day
7. the..........................sun
8. a.......................................hill
9. a..........................river
10. an....................................sum
11. an..........................face
12. a.......................................girl

(*b*) *Complete each sentence with a suitable* **adjective**:

1. We enjoyed a..........................................................sleep at night.
2. The woodcutter was very.................................................................
3. This is a very........................................................................knife.
4. A.......................................................fish was caught in the net.
5. Our fields give........................................................crops of wheat.
6. This story-book contains several.........................................pictures.
7. The.......................................................boy jumped into the river.
8. Mary's eyes are pretty and.............................................................
9. The girl has a ........................................................................voice.

## HOMEWORK

IV. *Here are some* **adjectives**. *Write the* **opposite** *of each:*

1. large .........................
2. sharp .........................
3. big .........................
4. heavy .........................
5. fat .........................
6. dirty .........................
7. old .........................
8. honest .........................
9. rich .........................
10. true .........................
11. tall .........................
12. long .........................

V. *Use each* **adjective** *in a sentence:*

1. ancient ..................................................
2. rude ..................................................
3. wealthy ..................................................
4. pleasant ..................................................
5. noisy ..................................................

VI. *Here is a list of ten words given in the box. Write each of them against the adjectives with the same meaning:*

| *wealthy* | *tidy* | *difficult* | *plump* | *beautiful* |
|---|---|---|---|---|
| *slim* | *high* | *small* | *lean* | *strong* |

| | | | |
|---|---|---|---|
| 1. thin | ........................ | 6. tough | ........................ |
| 2. weak | ........................ | 7. clean | ........................ |
| 3. rich | ........................ | 8. fat | ........................ |
| 4. little | ........................ | 9. tall | ........................ |
| 5. stout | ........................ | 10. pretty | ........................ |

VII. *What is an* **adjective***?*

..................................................................................................

..................................................................................................

VIII. *Read the passage and sort out the different* **adjectives** *used in it. Write them in the blanks given below:*

It is a simple but funny game. It is easy and cheap too. For it, you need a big table, two small balls and two narrow bowls. The teams stand on opposite sides of the table. Each player throws his ball into the bowl. Only good players can do it. The interesting game thus goes on. The team which finishes first is the winner.

................ ................ ................ ................ ................ ................

................ ................ ................ ................ ................ ................

(*10 different adjectives*)

# Lesson 16 : Verbs

## OBJECTIVES

To enable the pupils to know that —

- the word — verb — comes from an old French word verbe which means *word*.
- a verb is a word that stands for doing something or being something.
- in other words, a verb is a word that shows an action, an event or a fact.
- Verb is the most important word in a sentence. The other words in the sentence are linked to it.

## FACTS AND RULES

- Most of the verbs stand for actions, *i.e.* for doing something. So a verb is called a doing word, as:

  1. Children play in the park.
  2. Girls are dancing in the room.
  3. The cat has killed a rat.

- Verbs also show events that occur by themselves, as:

  1. The car failed on the way.
  2. It is raining heavily outside.
  3. The child fell off the roof.

- Verbs also express facts that are always true, as:

  1. The sun sets in the west.
  2. A bird has no teeth in its mouth.
  3. The sky is endless empty space.

- The verb is the most important word in a sentence. All the other words are linked to it. So it is called the soul of its sentence.
- A verb has three common forms as under :

  1. base form     2. past form     3. ing-form

- A verb is a word that shows an action, an event or a fact.

*Observe these pictures and the sentences below them:*

1. Alex **sings** a song.

2. The sun **rises** in the east.

3. Mother is **cooking** food.

4. Two cars **collided** with each other.

*We see that —*

1. The word '**sings**' shows the action of *singing*.
2. The word '**rises**' shows the fact of *sunrise*.
3. The words '**is cooking**' denote the action of *cooking*.
4. The word '**collided**' shows the event of *colliding*.

The words in bold type denote **actions, facts,** or **events**. Such words are called verbs.

**A verb is a word that denotes an action, an event or a fact.**

The verb is the most important word in a sentence. No sentence can be there without a verb. If a sentence is made up of only one word, it must be a verb. All the words of a sentence centre round its verb, as:

1. *Go*.
2. *Get up*.
3. *Come* to me.
4. Mothers *love* their babies.

# Practice Exercises

## CLASSWORK

I. *Sort out the* **verb** *in each sentence and write it in the blank given in front:*

1. Jack slept soundly. ..........................................
2. I am very happy. ..........................................
3. You run very fast. ..........................................
4. He does his work carefully. ..........................................
5. The peacock danced in the rain. ..........................................
6. She wrote a letter to me. ..........................................
7. The grass is green. ..........................................
8. We have a holiday tomorrow. ..........................................
9. I met an old beggar. ..........................................
10. There was an accident on the road. ..........................................

II. *Use these* **verbs** *in sentences:*

1. read : ..........................................................................................
2. write : ..........................................................................................
3. see : ..........................................................................................
4. hear : ..........................................................................................
5. play : ..........................................................................................
6. sleep : ..........................................................................................
7. sing : ..........................................................................................
8. dance : ..........................................................................................
9. drink : ..........................................................................................
10. weep : ..........................................................................................

III. *Write a suitable **verb** in each blank:*

1. The mother..........................................................................................food.
2. Fish..........................................................................................in water.
3. ..........................................................................................away from here.
4. The sun..........................................................................................in the east.
5. The moon..........................................................................................at night.
6. Birds ..........................................................................................in the air.
7. My grandma..........................................................................................us a story.
8. We..........................................................................a new lesson yesterday.
9. The dog is..........................................................................................
10. I..........................................................................................with my pen.
11. The aeroplane crashed while landing ..........................................in the sky.

## HOMEWORK

IV. *Each picture shows an action. Write the **verb** for it:*

..................................

..................................

..................................

..................................

..................................

..................................

V. *Use each* **verb** *in a sentence:*

1. grow : ..........................................................................
2. kill : ..........................................................................
3. go : ..........................................................................
4. speak : ..........................................................................
5. work : ..........................................................................
6. smell : ..........................................................................
7. bark : ..........................................................................
8. laugh : ..........................................................................
9. run : ..........................................................................
10. move : ..........................................................................
11. rise : ..........................................................................
12. sleep : ..........................................................................

VI. *Read this passage and write in the blanks the different* **verbs** *used in it:*

A man lived in a certain village. He had a goose. It laid a golden egg every day. The man was very greedy. He got only one egg at a time. He wanted all the eggs at one time. So he cut the goose open. How foolish he was! He wept bitterly at his folly.

.................................. .................................. ..................................

.................................. .................................. ..................................

.................................. .................................. *(8 different verbs)*

VII. *What is a* **verb**? *Give eight examples:*

..........................................................................................................

..........................................................................................................

*Examples:*

.......................... .......................... .......................... ..........................

.......................... .......................... .......................... ..........................

# Lesson 17 : Adverbs

## OBJECTIVES

To enable the pupils to know that —

- the word — adverb — means a word that adds something to the meaning of a verb.
- adverbs generally show the time, the place or the manner of doing an action.
- adverbs add to the meanings of adjectives and other adverbs also. They show the degree of the qualities shown by adjectives.
- like adjectives, adverbs are qualifying verbs. They qualify verbs, adjectives or other adverbs.

## FACTS AND RULES

- The word adverb is equal to add + verb, *i.e.* a word that adds something to the action shown by a verb, as:
  1. The sun is rising now. .........(now shows time of the action)
  2. The children are playing there. .........(there shows place of the action)
  3. The dog is barking loudly. .........(loudly shows manner of the action)
  4. Peter is a very strong boy. .........(very shows degree of the adj. strong)
- It is clear that —
  1. An adverb showing the time of an action is an adverb of time, as:
     (*a*) I get up early to go for a walk. (*b*) You should never tell lies.
     (*c*) We shall go boating today. (*d*) What will you do now?
  2. An adverb showing the place of an action is an adverb of place, as:
     (*a*) Place those books here. (*b*) Where are you coming from?
     (*c*) There is was a pool near by. (*d*) Whither will you go now?
  3. An adverb showing the manner of an action is an adverb of manner, as:
     (*a*) The child is weeping bitterly. (*b*) Our soldiers fought bravely.
     (*c*) Do your homework carefully. (*d*) The sun is shining brightly.
  4. An adverb showing the degree of a quality is an adverb of degree, as:
     (*a*) The light of the full moon is very *cool*.
     (*b*) The light of the summer sun is extremely *hot*.
     (*c*) Susan dresses quite *neatly*.

## ADVERBS

*Observe these sentences:*

1. *Do* it **at once**.
2. Ask him to *sit* **here**.
3. It is *raining* **heavily.**
4. He is working **very** *hard*.
5. Do your work **most** *carefully*.

*We see that —*

1. **at once** shows the *time* of doing the action.
2. **here** shows the *place* of the action of *sitting*.
3. **heavily** shows the manner of the action of *raining*.
4. **very** shows the degree of *hardness*.
5. **most** shows the degree of *being careful*.

All the words in bold type are qualifying words. They qualify verbs or adjectives. In the case of verbs, the qualifying words show time or place, or manner of doing an action. In the case of adjectives, they show the degree of a quality. All these qualifying words are called **adverbs**.

**Adverbs are words that qualify verbs or adjectives/adverbs.**

# Practice Exercises

## CLASSWORK

I. *Sort out* **adverbs** *and write them in the blanks:*

1. He did not live happily. ..........................................
2. He often comes to see me. ..........................................
3. They fought very bravely. ..........................................
4. We must always speak the truth. ..........................................

5. The moon is shining brightly. ..........................................

6. She always dresses neatly. .................... ,....................

7. The lady wept bitterly. ..........................................

8. We killed the snake then and there. ..........................................

9. I get up early and go for a walk. ..........................................

10. She talks politely. .................... , ....................

11. Tim and Kim sing sweetly. ..........................................

12. The dog was barking very loudly. .................... , ....................

II. *Write a suitable* **adverb** *for each verb:*

| | | | | | |
|---|---|---|---|---|---|
| 1. | talk | ............................ | 2. | fight | ............................ |
| 3. | sing | ............................ | 4. | love | ............................ |
| 5. | write | ............................ | 6. | roar | ............................ |
| 7. | work | ............................ | 8. | read | ............................ |
| 9. | run | ............................ | 10. | move | ............................ |
| 11. | stop | ............................ | 12. | treat | ............................ |
| 13. | shine | ............................ | 14. | rain | ............................ |
| 15. | act | ............................ | 16. | sleep | ............................ |
| 17. | look | ............................ | 18. | walk | ............................ |
| 19. | hear | ............................ | 20. | speak | ............................ |

III. *Fill in each blank with an* **adverb**:

1. They welcomed us....................................................................................
2. You should..............................................................................tell a lie.
3. We must...........................................................................speak truth.
4. Finish this work now and..........................................................................
5. The moon crossed the sky..........................................................................

6. You must speak..........................................................................to others.
7. She looked...................................................................at my face.
8. The child was weeping..........................................................................
9. I............................................................................go to see him.
10. We do our homework.......................................................carefully.
11. The lion roared..................................................inside the cage.
12. The robber killed the traveller.......................................cruelly.

## HOMEWORK

IV. *Use these* **adverbs** *in sentences:*

1. carefully : ..............................................................................
2. angrily : ..............................................................................
3. happily : ..............................................................................
4. politely : ..............................................................................
5. gently : ..............................................................................
6. yesterday : ..............................................................................
7. often : ..............................................................................
8. seldom : ..............................................................................
9. there : ..............................................................................
10. noisily : ..............................................................................

V. *Given below are six adverbs in a box. Write each of them against the adverb with a similar meaning.*

| *harshly* | *lovingly* | *ever* | *quietly* | *unhappily* | *politely* |
|---|---|---|---|---|---|

1. gently
2. roughly
3. affectionately
4. always
5. sadly
6. silently

VI. *Given below are ten adverbs in a box. Write each of them against the adverb with an opposite meaning.*

| *politely* | *quickly* | *sadly* | *lovingly* | *noisily* |
|---|---|---|---|---|
| *boldly* | *ever* | *then* | *often* | *carefully* |

| | | | | | |
|---|---|---|---|---|---|
| 1. | rudely | .................... | 6. | gladly | .................... |
| 2. | angrily | .................... | 7. | seldom | .................... |
| 3. | quietly | .................... | 8. | never | .................... |
| 4. | timidly | .................... | 9. | carelessly | .................... |
| 5. | slowly | .................... | 10. | now | .................... |

VII. *What is an* **adverb**? *Write four sentences as examples of adverbs of time, place, manner and degree respectively:*

Adverb : ..............................................................................................

..............................................................................................

*Examples:*

1. .............................................................................................. (*time*)
2. .............................................................................................. (*place*)
3. .............................................................................................. (*manner*)
4. .............................................................................................. (*degree*)

VIII. *Read this passage and write the different* **adverbs** *used in it, in the blanks:*

When we reached there, they welcomed us warmly. They offered us food and talked to us politely. We stayed with them comfortably. We have returned here today. We would like to revisit them tomorrow.

.................................... .................................... ....................................

.................................... .................................... ....................................

.................................... .................................... (*8 different verbs*)

# Lesson 18 : Prepositions

## OBJECTIVES

To enable the pupils to know that —

- the word — preposition = pre (before) + position = position before something.
- a preposition is a small word that is placed before a noun/pronoun.
- a preposition used before a noun/pronoun links it with another noun/pronoun used in the same sentence.

## FACTS AND RULES

- A preposition is a small word that is used to show the position of a noun/pronoun in terms of place/time, as:

| | | | | | |
|---|---|---|---|---|---|
| in | = inside | out | = outside | under | = on the lower side |
| near | = close to | before | = in front | over | = on the upper side |
| behind | = on the back | of | = owned by | between | = flanked by |

- Also, a preposition is a word that is positioned before a noun or pronoun, as:

| | | |
|---|---|---|
| in a park | on a shelf | under a table |
| over the wall | before sunrise | after sunset |

- A preposition, when used in a sentence, links two nouns, two pronouns or a noun and a pronoun, as:

1. The *goat* ran down the *hill*. .......(goat, hill).......(*two nouns*)
2. *I* was helped by *him*. ...........(I, him)....... (*two pronouns*)
3. This *apple is* for *you*. ....(apple, you)...... (a *noun and a pronoun*)

- Some common simple prepositions are as given below:

| | | | | | | |
|---|---|---|---|---|---|---|
| after | at | by | down | for | from | in |
| near | of | off | on | out | over | round |
| since | through | till | to | under | up | with |

- Some common compound prepositions are as given below:

| | | | | | | |
|---|---|---|---|---|---|---|
| about | above | across | before | behind | below | between |
| inside | into | onto | outside | until | within | without |

## PREPOSITIONS

Some sentences have more-than-one nouns or pronouns used in them. These nouns or pronouns are joined to one another by small words.

*Observe the following sentences:*

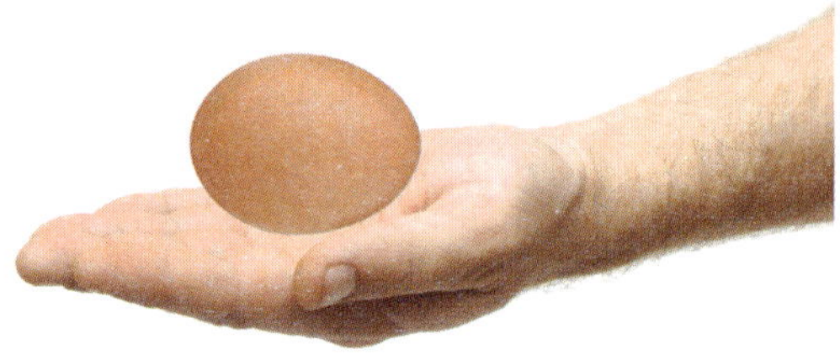

1. The *egg* is **on** the *hand*.
2. The *basket* is **under** the *table*.
3. I gave a *pen* **to** *him*.
4. *Children* are **in** the *park*.
5. *Boys* **of** this *school* are naughty.

*We see that—*

1. The word '**on'** shows the link between the *egg* and the *hand*.
2. The word '**under**' shows the link between the nouns *basket* and the *table*.
3. The word '**to**' shows the link between the noun *pen* and the pronoun *him*.
4. The word '**in**' shows the link between the nouns — *children, park*.
5. The word '**of**' shows the link between the nouns — *boys, school*.

Each of these words — *on, under, to, in, of* — governs the link/relation between nouns and pronouns in the same sentence. Such words are called **prepositions**.

**A preposition is a word placed before a noun or a pronoun to show its relation to some other noun or pronoun in the same sentence.**

Here is a list of some common prepositions:

*across, above, after, about, among, off, beside, by, before, between, behind, below, down, during, from, for, near, in, into, of, on, over, since, through, under, until, up, upon, with, within, without, round, onto, till, beyond, past.*

# Practice Exercises

## CLASSWORK

I. *Sort out the* **prepositions** *and write them in the blanks:*

1. The cat is sitting on the mat. ..............................
2. The boys are in the room. ..............................
3. The dog jumped over the fence. ..............................
4. Pour tea into the cup. ..............................

5. We are anxious about it. ..............................
6. He stood beside the door. ..............................
7. The sun shines during the day. ..............................
8. This apple is not for you. ..............................

9. Leaves fall off the trees in autumn. ..............................
10. John was looking for his friend. ..............................
11. They drove through the bazaar. ..............................
12. The goat ran down the hill. ..............................
13. You must be back before dusk. ..............................

14. We cannot do without food. ..............................
15. Look at the blackboard. ..............................
16. The hut is made of wood. ..............................

17. My friend swam across the river. ..............................
18. He stands between Jack and Jane. ..............................

II. *Fill in each blank with a suitable* **preposition**:

1. The cat ran..............................................................................the rat.
2. I played..............................................................................a bat and a ball.
3. I bought this pen..............................................................................two rupees.

4. Fill red ink................................................................the pen.
5. Mr David prefers to work..................................................a farm.
6. The way lay..........................................................a dense forest.
7. My head is..........................................................my shoulders.
8. A stream lay...............................................the road to the town.
9. The sheep ran.......................................................the hillside.
10. Can we do..................................................food and clothes?
11. My school is just..............................................the bus-stop.
12. Rosy reaches school.............................................9 o'clock.

III. *Use each of these* **prepositions** *in a sentence:*

1. at : ........................................................................
2. of : ........................................................................
3. under : ........................................................................
4. from : ........................................................................
5. before : ........................................................................
6. down : ........................................................................
7. over : ........................................................................
8. beside : ........................................................................
9. on : ........................................................................
10. near : ........................................................................
11. after : ........................................................................
12. behind : ........................................................................
13. above : ........................................................................
14. in : ........................................................................
15. into : ........................................................................

## HOMEWORK

IV. *Sort out the* **prepositions** *and write them in the blanks:*

1. They passed through a thick forest. ..............................
2. The drawer of the table is narrow. ..............................
3. You must act upon his advice. ..............................
4. The chair is behind the table. ..............................
5. There is a bridge over the river. ..............................
6. He fell off the roof suddenly. .............. , ...........
7. We go for a walk every day. .............. , ...........
8. I will tell you about my plan. .............. , ...........

V. *What is a* **preposition**?

..............................................................................................................

..............................................................................................................

VI. *Use these* **prepositions** *in sentences:*

I. near : ..........................................................................................
2. at : ..........................................................................................
3. through : ..........................................................................................
4. with : ..........................................................................................
5. after : ..........................................................................................
6. below : ..........................................................................................
7. down : ..........................................................................................
8. before : ..........................................................................................
9. round : ..........................................................................................

VII. *Read this passage and write the different* **prepositions** *used in it:*

Mark was suffering from cold and cough. He kept sneezing into the hanky he carried in his hand. His mother took him to a doctor. Mark sat on a chair beside a table. There was a cat sitting under the chair. Mark got scared and ran inside the doctor's cabin.

.................................. .................................. ..................................

.................................. .................................. ..................................

.................................. .................................. (*8 different prepositions*)

VIII. *Look at each picture carefully and choose the correct* **preposition** *from the given options to complete the sentence under it.*

Fruits are .................. the basket.
(*in, on, under*)

A cat is .................. the box.
(*in, on, inside*)

The shoes are.................. the bed.
(*in, on, under*)

A shirt hangs .................. the hanger.
(*in, on, from*)

# Lesson 19 : Conjunctions

## OBJECTIVES

To enable the pupils to know that —

- the word — conjunction = con (together) + junction = (joining) = joining together.
- a conjunction is a word that joins together words, word-groups or sentences.
- some conjunctions join together words or sentences of similar nature.
- some conjunctions join together words or sentences of opposite nature.
- some conjunctions join together words or sentences that show alternative choices.
- some conjunctions join together words or sentences and show that one of the two is the result of the other.

## FACTS AND RULES

- A conjunction is a word that joins together words, word-groups or sentences, as:

  *a spoon* and *a fork* *young* yet *wise* *by bus* or *by car*

  1. *He is very weak* so *he cannot walk.* 2. *I was absent*, because *I was ill.*

- Words and sentences of similar nature are joined by conjunctions like and, as :

  1. The king was *old* and *weak.* 2. The queen was *fair* as well as *charming.*

- Words and sentences of the opposite nature are joined by conjunctions like but, as:

  1. The soldier was *strong* but *timid.*
  2. The king was *old* yet *active.*
  3. I *walked fast,* still I *got late.*
  4. He *cannot dance* however *hard he may try.*

- Words and sentences showing a choice are joined by conjunctions like or, as:

  1. You may go *by bus* or *by train.*
  2. Let us make a *do* or *die* effort.
  3. *Walk fast* otherwise *we shall be late.*
  4. Hand over your money else *be ready to die.*

- Words and sentences showing that one is the result of the other, are joined by conjunctions like so, therefore, as:

  1. I *am unwell,* therefore I cannot *come to school.*
  2. He is *very weak,* so he cannot *walk properly.*
  3. He was punished because he was late.

## CONJUNCTIONS

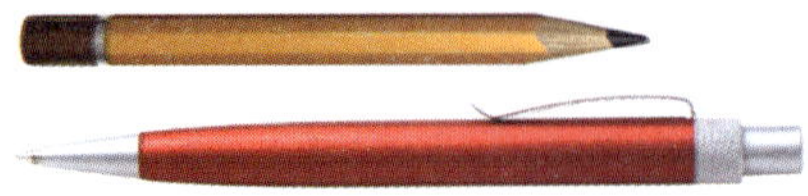

*Observe the following sentences:*

1. I have a pen. I have a pencil.
   I have a pen **and** a pencil.
2. Betty is tall. Lucy is short.
   Betty is tall **but** Lucy is short.
3. She cannot walk. She is very weak.
   She cannot walk **since** she is very weak.
4. Walk fast. You will be late.
   Walk fast **else** you will be late.

*We see that —*

1. In sentence 1, the word '**and**' joins two similar words — *pen* and *pencil*.
2. In sentence 2, the word '**but**' joins two such sentence that state opposite facts.
3. In sentence 3, the word '**since**' joins *two such sentences* that one is the result of the other.
4. In sentence 4, the word '**else**' joins such sentences that show a choice.

The words — *and, but, since, else* — are joining words. They join words and sentences. Such words are called **conjunctions**.

**A conjunction is a word that joins together words, groups of words or sentences.**

Here is a list of words commonly used as conjunctions:

| | | | | |
|---|---|---|---|---|
| lest | and | unless | whether | or |
| else | yet | until/till | otherwise | before |
| that | if | still | though | after |
| since/for | but | however | because | while |

# Practice Exercises

## CLASSWORK

I. *Sort out the* **conjunctions** *and write them in the blanks given in front*:

1. Harry is intelligent as well as active. ..................................
2. I have a loving and kind mother. ..................................
3. She ran hard yet she came second. ..................................
4. Walk quickly else we shall be late. ..................................
5. Use an umbrella because it is raining. ..................................
6. He is honest though he is poor. ..................................
7. He is timid but his brother is bold. ..................................
8. Walk slowly lest you should fall. ..................................
9. You should exercise else you will be weak. ..................................
10. Work hard otherwise you will fail. ..................................

II. *Fill in each blank with a* **conjunction**:

1. Peter is clever..........................................................................strong.
2. Tom is intelligent.......................................................................... he is idle.
3. Work hard..........................................................................you will fail.
4. He is rich..........................................................................he is dishonest.
5. I fell off the roof,..........................................................................I was not hurt.
6. He cannot hear..........................................................................he is deaf.
7. She is tall .......................................................................... her sister is short.
8. Do not trust him..........................................................................he is a rogue.

III. *What is a* **conjunction**?

..........................................................................................................................................

..........................................................................................................................................

## HOMEWORK

IV. *Use each of these* **conjunctions** *in a sentence:*

1. and : ..........................................................................
2. but : ..........................................................................
3. yet : ..........................................................................
4. so : ..........................................................................
5. while : ..........................................................................
6. because : ..........................................................................

V. *Sort out* **conjunctions** *and write them in the blanks:*

1. Susan is intelligent and hardworking. ..............................
2. Tell me the truth else I shall not talk to you. ..............................
3. I must help you since you are my friend. ..............................
4. You are weak, so you must eat good food. ..............................
5. He finished early though he had started late. ..............................
6. Walk carefully lest you should stumble. ..............................

VI. *Join each set of sentences using a* **conjunction**:

1. He is poor. He is happy.

   ..........................................................................

2. I bought a shirt. I bought shorts.

   ..........................................................................

3. He went to the market. He bought vegetables.

   ..........................................................................

4. He did not work hard. He has failed.

   ..........................................................................

5. You must start soon. You will be late.

   ..........................................................................

# Lesson 20 : Interjections

## OBJECTIVES

To enable the pupils to know that —

- the word — interjection = inter (in between) + jection = (driving) = driving in between.
- an interjection is a word that is driven into speech suddenly under a strong feeling.
- an interjection is exclaimed aloud suddenly while saying something.
- interjections stand for different feelings that are given below:

| | | | |
|---|---|---|---|
| joy | sorrow | anger | surprise |
| praise | hate | rebuke | attention |
| a blessing | a curse | encouragement | dislike |

## FACTS AND RULES

- An interjection is a word that is suddenly exclaimed during a speech under a strong feeling, as:

1. Bravo! what a nice hit!
2. Hurrah! mom has come.
3. Hush! the baby is asleep.
4. Hello! what brings you here?

- There are different interjections for different feelings, as:

| *Interjection* | *Feeling* | *Interjection* | *Feeling* | *Interjection* | *Feeling* |
|---|---|---|---|---|---|
| Hurrah ! | joy | Ha ! | approval | Oh ! | regret |
| Alas ! | sorrow | Hello ! | address | Hush ! | caution |
| Lo ! | attention | Ouch ! | pain | Pooh ! | hate |
| Fie ! | dislike | Bravo ! | bucking up | My Goodness ! | wonder |

- Each interjection is followed by the sign (!)
- If the interjection is a single word, the sentence after it starts with a small letter.

1. Alas! my friend is no more.
2. Hurrah! we have won the match.
3. Pooh! what a dirty child!
4. Fie! how mean you are!
5. Oh! what a fool I am!
6. Hello! how are you, Peter?

- If the exclamation is a full sentence, the sentence after it starts with a capital letter.

1. How mean you are! Nobody shall bear you.
2. What a lovely child! Only if it were my son!

## INTERJECTIONS

*Observe these sentences:*

1. **Hurrah!** our team has won the match.
2. **Alas!** my cat is no more.
3. **Hello!** how do you do, David?
4. **Oh!** how silly of me !
5. **Bravo!** you have done very well.
6. **Ha!** what a charming scenery!

*We see that —*

1. The word '**Hurrah**' expresses a sudden feeling of *joy*.
2. The word '**Alas**' expresses a sudden feeling of *sorrow*.
3. The word '**Hello**' expresses a feeling of *getting attention*.
4. The word '**Oh**' expresses a sudden feeling of *regret*.
5. The word '**Bravo**' expresses a sudden feeling of *praise*.
6. The word '**Ha**' expresses a sudden feeling of *approval*.

## MARK OF EXCLAMATION

All these words in bold type '*Hurrah, Alas, Hello, Oh, Bravo and Ha*' express sudden feelings. So they are called **interjections**.

**An interjection is a word that expresses a sudden feeling.**

Here are some other common interjections:

*Fie!* *Pooh!* *Hush!* *Ouch!* *Lo!*

An interjection is always followed by the sign (!). As interjections are always exclaimed, this sign is called an **exclamation mark**.

Remember that the sentence after the mark of exclamation normally starts with a small letter. It starts with a capital letter if the exclamation mark comes at the end of the previous sentence.

# Practice Exercises

## CLASSWORK

I. *Sort out* **interjections** *and write them in the blanks:*

1. Hurrah! daddy has come. ................................
2. Hello! what brings you here? ................................
3. Fie! she is so dishonest. ................................
4. Alas! our friend is no more. ................................
5. Oh! that was silly of you. ................................
6. Aha! what a pretty flower! ................................
7. Hush! someone is coming. ................................
8. Lo! here comes your papa. ................................

## HOMEWORK

II. *Put a suitable* **interjection** *in each blank:*

1. ....................................................................! we have lost the match.
2. ....................................................................! well played.
3. ....................................................................! how sweet a song!
4. ....................................................................! how ugly she looks!
5. ....................................................................! how are you?
6. ....................................................................! do not speak aloud.
7. ....................................................................! how mean of him!
8. ....................................................................! daddy has come.

III. *What is an* **interjection**?

....................................................................................................

....................................................................................................

# Lesson 21 : Parsing

**OBJECTIVE**

- To enable the pupils to describe the grammar of each word of a sentence.

**FACTS AND RULES**

- Each word of a sentence is a different part of speech. Verbs, adjectives, determiners, adverbs, prepositions, conjunctions and interjections can be sorted out easily.
- Nouns/pronouns are different in number, gender and person.
- To break a sentence in its words and to explain their grammar is called parsing.

*Observe this sentence:*

**John is a naughty boy but a good student.**

*In this sentence:*

1. **John** — is a **singular noun** of *masculine gender* and *third person*.
2. **is** — is a **verb** *of the present tense.*
3. **a** — is a **determiner**.
4. **naughty** — is an **adjective** qualifying the noun *boy*.
5. **boy** — is a **noun** of *singular number* and *masculine gender*.
6. **but** — is a **conjunction** joining words of opposite nature.
7. **good** — is an **adjective** qualifying the noun *student*.
8. **student** — is a **singular noun** of *common gender* and *third person*.

Each word of the sentence given above has been explained in terms of grammar. This process is called **parsing**.

**Parsing is the process of breaking up a sentence into words and explaining their grammar.**

## Practice Exercises

*Parse each sentence:*

1. We need clothes and food.
2. The gardener is watering the plants.
3. The dog is a faithful animal.
4. Bad children have dirty habits.
5. Bravo ! you have played well.
6. Beauty cannot be bought with money.

# Lesson 22 : Questions and Answers

## OBJECTIVES

- To enable the pupils to know that speaking is important for learning a language.
- A language can be learnt through conversation — talking to others.
- Common question words used in English conversation are — what, which, who, whom, whose, why, when, where, how, how many and how often.
- Learning how to answer questions is a must for learning how to speak English.

### A. WHAT

| Questions | Answers |
|---|---|
| 1. What is your name? | My name is Sam. |
| 2. What does your father do? | My father is a doctor. |
| 3. What are you? | I am a human being. |
| 4. What is the colour of your shirt? | My shirt is red. |
| 5. What is your age? | I am ten years old. |

### B. WHO, WHOM, WHOSE

| Questions | Answers |
|---|---|
| 1. Who are you? | I am Peter. |
| 2. Who is your class teacher? | Mr Derek is my class teacher. |
| 3. Whom do you want to see? | I want to see Mr Jack. |
| 4. Whose pen is this? | This pen is mine. |

### C. WHICH

| Questions | Answers |
|---|---|
| 1. Which is your book? | This is my book. |
| 2. Which book is yours? | This book is mine. |
| 3. Which class are you in? | I am in class III. |
| 4. Which of these is the better? | This is the better. |

### D. WHY, WHERE, WHEN

| Questions | Answers |
|---|---|
| 1. Why are you late? | Because I missed the bus. |
| 2. Where do you live? | I live in Tokyo. |
| 3. Where do you come from? | I come from a village. |
| 4. When do you get up? | I get up at 5:00 a.m. |
| 5. When do you go to bed? | I go to bed at 10:00 p.m. |

## E. HOW, HOW MANY, etc.

| | | |
|---|---|---|
| 1. | How do you come to school? | I come to school on foot. |
| 2. | How tall are you? | I am 105 cm. tall. |
| 3. | How many brothers have you got? | I have got two brothers. |
| 4. | How many brothers are you? | We are three brothers. |
| 5. | How often do you eat daily? | I eat thrice a day. |

# Practice Exercises

## CLASSWORK

*Answer these questions:*

1. How heavy are you? ..............................................................................
2. Who is your father? ..............................................................................
3. What colour is the sky? ..............................................................................
4. What is a knife for? ..............................................................................
5. What does your father do?..............................................................................

## HOMEWORK

1. How many sister have you got?

   ..............................................................................

2. Which standard are you in?

   ..............................................................................

3. What colour are your shoes?

   ..............................................................................

4. How far is your school from your house?

   ..............................................................................

5. How often do you take tea daily?

   ..............................................................................

# SECTION II —VOCABULARY

## I. DAYS OF THE WEEK

Sunday Monday Tuesday Wednesday Thursday Friday Saturday

**Weekdays:** Monday, Tuesday, Wednesday, Thursday, Friday

**Weekends:** Saturday, Sunday

**Fortnight:** fourteen nights, *i.e.* two weeks

## II. MONTHS OF THE YEAR

To begin with, a year was divided into **10 months.** It is clear from the following names—

| | | | |
|---|---|---|---|
| **September** | 7th month | **October** | eighth month |
| **November** | 9th month | **December** | Tenth month |

Later on, two great emperors of Rome added two months. Emperor *Julius Caesar* added the month of **July** and *Emperor Augustus* added the month of **August**. So the year came to have twelve months as under :

| Month | Days | Month | Days | Month | Days |
|---|---|---|---|---|---|
| January | 31 | February | 28/29 | March | 31 |
| April | 30 | May | 31 | June | 30 |
| July | 31 | August | 31 | September | 30 |
| October | 31 | November | 30 | December | 31 |

**Learn this verse:**

Thirty days have September, April, June and November.

All the others have one and thirty, February has eight and twenty.

## III. SUBJECTS

| | | | |
|---|---|---|---|
| English | Hindi | History | Social Studies |
| Mathematics | Geography | Drawing | General Science |
| Grammar | Language | Civics | Moral Science |

## IV. GAMES AND SPORTS

| | | |
|---|---|---|
| badminton | boxing | blindman's buff |
| cricket | football | hide-and-seek |
| tip-cat | leap frog | ping-pong |
| tennis | hockey | volley-ball |
| carom | cards | chess |

A pack of cards has *52 cards*.
It has four sets of cards. Each set has *13 cards*.
Each set of cards is given a name as under.

| | | | |
|---|---|---|---|
| *Diamonds* | ♦ | *Clubs* | ♣ |
| *Hearts* | ♥ | *Spades* | ♠ |

## CRIES OF ANIMALS

| Animal | Cry | Animal | Cry |
|---|---|---|---|
| Apes | gibber | Geese | cackel |
| Asses | bray | Hens | cluck |
| Bears | growl | Horses | neigh |
| Bees | hum | Hyaenas | laugh |
| Birds | chirp | Jackals | howl |
| Bulls | bellow | Kangaroos | chortle |
| Goats/sheep | bleat | Koalas | wail |
| Camels | grunt | Lions | roar |
| Cats | mew, purr | Lambs | bleat |
| Cows | moo | Mice | squeak |
| Cocks | crow | Monkeys | chatter |
| Crows | caw | Nightingales | warble |
| Dogs | bark | Owls | hoot |
| Ducks | quack | Parrots | talk |
| Eagles | scream | Pigs | grunt |
| Elephants | trumpet | Snakes | hiss |
| Flies | buzz | Tigers | growl |

## VI. YOUNG ONES OF ANIMALS

| Animal | Young one | Animal | Young one |
|---|---|---|---|
| Ass/Donkey | Foal | Goose | Gosling |
| Bear | Cub | Hen | Chicken |
| Bird | Chick | Horse | Colt/Filly |
| Buffalo | Calf | Hyena | Cub |
| Camel | Calf | Kangaroo | Joey |
| Cat | Kitten | Leopard | Cub |
| Cheetah | Cub | Lion | Cub |
| Cock | Cockerel | Monkey | Infant |
| Dog | Pup | Mule | Foal |
| Deer | Fawn | Owl | Owlet |
| Duck | Duckling | Pig | Piglet |
| Eagle | Eaglet | Rabbit | Bunny/Kit |
| Elephant | Calf | Sheep | Lamb |
| Fish | Fry/Fingerling | Snake | Snakelet |
| Fox | Cub/Pup | Swan | Cygnet |
| Frog | Tadpole | Whale | Calf |
| Goat | Kid/Billy | Yak | Calf |

## VII. HOMES

| Creature | Home | Creature | Home |
|---|---|---|---|
| King | Palace | Nun | Convent |
| Man | House | Prisoner | Prison |
| Monk | Monastery | Soldier | Barrack |
| Bird | Nest | Cow | Shed |
| Dog | Kennel | Hare | Form |
| Hen | Coop | Horse | Stable |
| Lion | Den | Mouse | Burrow |
| Bee | Hive | Sheep | Pen |
| Snake | Nest/Burrow | Spider | Cobweb |

## VIII. MEALS

| | | |
|---|---|---|
| **breakfast** | : | the first light meal of the day |
| **luncheon** | : | the meal at noon (called *lunch)* |
| **brunch** | : | a heavy meal to cover breakfast and lunch |
| **dinner** | : | the meal in the evening |
| **supper** | : | the meal late in the night |

## IX. OCCUPATIONS

| | | |
|---|---|---|
| **actor** | : | a person who acts on the stage |
| **artist** | : | a person who practises a fine art |
| **author** | : | a person who writes books |
| **artisan** | : | a person who practises a craft |
| **barber** | : | a person who does hair-cuts |
| **butcher** | : | a person who sells meat |
| **carpenter** | : | a person who works with wood |
| **chemist** | : | a person who sells medicines |
| **cobbler** | : | a person who mends shoes |
| **chauffeur** | : | a professional driver |
| **florist** | : | a person who sells flowers |
| **fruiterer** | : | a person who sells fruit |
| **grocer** | : | a person who sells provisions/grocery |
| **greengrocer** | : | a person who sells vegetables |
| **glazier** | : | a person who does glass-work |
| **juggler** | : | a person who shows feats |
| **locksmith** | : | a person who repairs locks |
| **ironsmith** | : | a person who works with iron |
| **goldsmith** | : | a person who makes ornaments |
| **mason** | : | a person who builds houses |
| **porter** | : | a person who carries luggage |

## X. THINGS WHERE MADE

| Thing | Where Made | Thing | Where Made |
|---|---|---|---|
| bread | bakery | bricks | kiln |
| money | mint | ships | shipyard |
| vests | hosiery | medicines | pharmacy |
| food | kitchen | films | studio |
| flour | mill | leather | tannery |

## XI. THINGS WHERE KEPT

| Thing | Where Kept | Thing | Where Kept |
|---|---|---|---|
| bird | cage | goods | godown |
| garbage | filth | books | shelf |
| plants | nursery | clothes | wardrobe |

## XII. GAMES WHERE PLAYED

| Game | Where Played | Game | Where Played |
|---|---|---|---|
| chess | board | boxing | ring |
| golf | course | tennis | court |
| carom | board | skating | rink |
| hockey | field | cricket | pitch |
| race | course | football | ground |

## XIII. SMALLER PIECES

1. a **crumb** of bread
2. a **puff** of wind
3. a **sip** of milk
4. a **grain** of sand
5. a **chip** of wood
6. a **wink** of sleep
7. a **morsel** of food
8. a **pinch** of salt
9. a **scrap** of paper
10. a **drop** of water

## XIV. COMMON DISEASES

1. asthma (pronounced *azma*)
2. malaria
3. cholera
4. typhoid
5. influenza
6. polio
7. smallpox
8. tuberculosis (T.B.)
9. fever

## XV. WORDS WRITTEN TOGETHER

1. instead
2. almost
3. cannot
4. almighty
5. already
6. although
7. wherein
8. whereof
9. wherefrom
10. into
11. onto
12. whereto

## XVI. WORDS WRITTEN SEPARATE

1. per cent
2. all right
3. at least
4. for ever
5. at most
6. all round
7. some one
8. no one
9. in spite of

## XVII. AVOID THESE PITFALLS

(a) Never put a full-stop after **Mr** and **Mrs**

(b) Never write **cannot** as *can not*

(c) Never write **all right** as *alright*

(d) Never write **already** as *all ready*

(e) Never write **into** as *in to.*

## XVIII. COMMON PHRASES

| | | | | |
|---|---|---|---|---|
| 1. | **get up** | to rise | : | I get up at 5:00 a.m. every day. |
| 2. | **put on** | to wear | : | Put on your school uniform. |
| 3. | **take off** | to remove | : | I took off my hat. |
| 4. | **give up** | to leave | : | Give up all your bad habits. |
| 5. | **leave for** | to go | : | He is leaving for London soon. |
| 6. | **go through** | to read | : | I have **gone through** this book. |

| | | | | |
|---|---|---|---|---|
| 7. | **get through** | to pass | : | She will **get through** the test. |
| 8. | **bring up** | to rear | : | Parents **bring up** their children. |
| 9. | **look after** | take care of | : | Mothers **look after** the homes. |
| 10. | **get into** | to be in | : | He has **got into** bad company. |

## XIV. COMMON PROVERBS

1. After lunch rest a while, after dinner walk a mile.
2. An apple a day, keeps the doctor away.
3. Bad money drives out good.
4. Bad news travels fast.
5. A bad workman blames his tools.
6. Beauty is only skin-deep.
7. It is all for the best.
8. Always be ready for the worst.
9. Better late than never.
10. Blood is thicker than water.

## XX. A CROSSWORD PUZZLE

### Across

1. Fourteen nights
2. A lion lives in a .............
3. This subject tells us about the past

### Down

1. Month with 28/29 days
4. A nun lives in a ...............
5. A baby-cat.

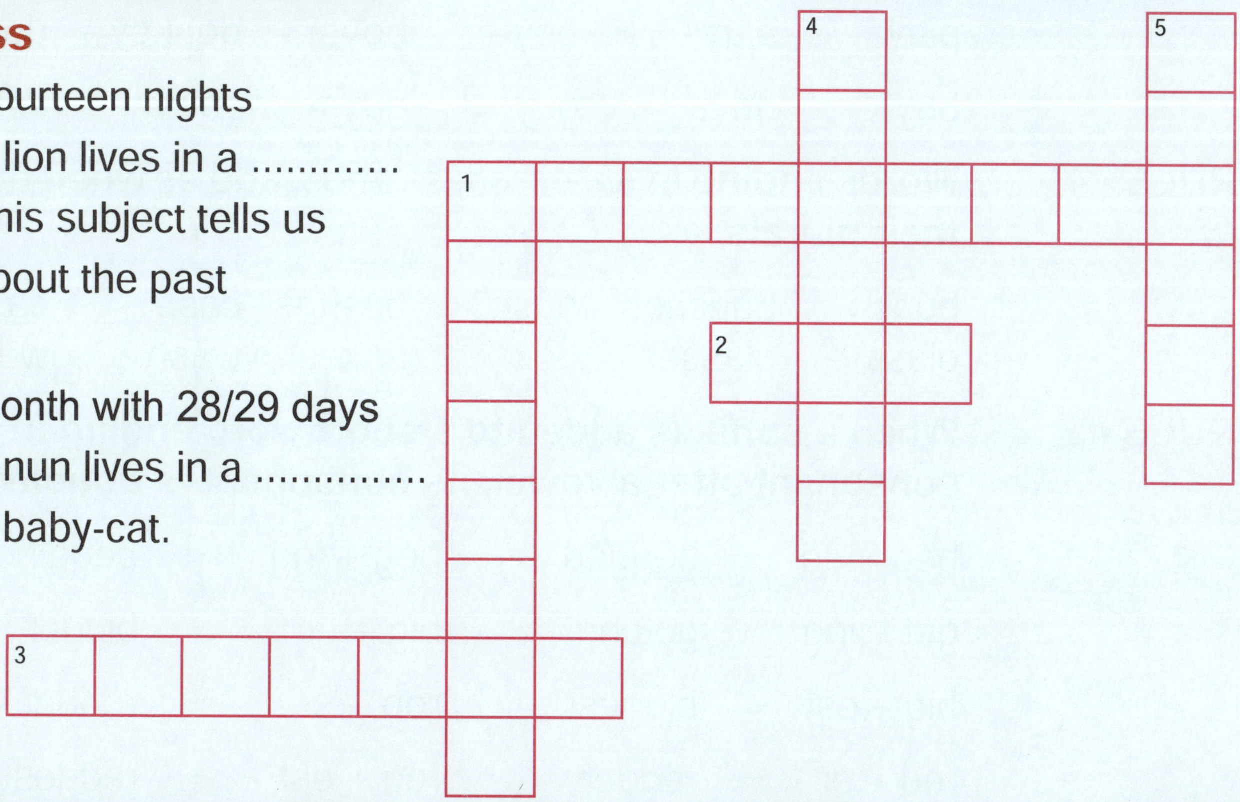

# SECTION III : SPELLING AND PRONUNCIATION

## A – SPELLING

As far as spelling is concerned, the English language is full of exceptions. Still there are some rules that can help us a lot. Let us study these rules:

**RULE - 1 :** **Verbs ending in** *e* **drop it when** *ing* **is added to them, as:**

| | | | | | |
|---|---|---|---|---|---|
| come + ing | = | coming | hope + ing | = | hoping |
| blame + ing | = | blaming | state + ing | = | stating |

But learn these **exceptions:**

| | | | | | |
|---|---|---|---|---|---|
| dye + ing | = | dyeing | lie + ing | = | lying |
| flee + ing | = | fleeing | see + ing | = | seeing |

**RULE - 2 :** **When a word ends in** *y* **after a consonant,** *y* **changes into** *ie* **when** *s* **is added to the word,** as:

| | | | | | |
|---|---|---|---|---|---|
| baby | babies | lady | ladies | body | bodies |
| party | parties | carry | carries | marry | marries |

**RULE - 3 :** **When a word ends in** *y* **after a vowel,** *y* **does not change when** *s* **is added to the word,** as:

| | | | | | |
|---|---|---|---|---|---|
| play | plays | boy | boys | donkey | donkeys |
| buy | buys | guy | guys | valley | valleys |

**RULE - 4 :** **Words ending in** *ch*, *es*, *sh*, *ss* **and** *x* **add** *es* **when they form their plurals,** as:

| | | | | | |
|---|---|---|---|---|---|
| bunch | bunches | bush | bushes | case | cases |
| glass | glasses | box | boxes | wash | washes |

**RULE - 5 :** **When a suffix is added to a short word ending in a consonant after a vowel, its consonant is doubled,** as:

| | | | | | |
|---|---|---|---|---|---|
| beg + ed | = | begged | beg + ing | = | begging |
| get + ing | = | getting | big + er | = | bigger |
| big + est | = | biggest | rob + er | = | robber |
| red + er | = | redder | red + est | = | reddest |

**RULE - 6 : When *full* is suffixed to a word, its *one l* is dropped, as:**

| | | | | | |
|---|---|---|---|---|---|
| thank + full | = | thankful | right + full | = | rightful |
| hand + full | = | handful | need + full | = | needful |

**RULE - 7 : When *all* is prefixed to any word, it drops its *one l*, as:**

| | | | | | |
|---|---|---|---|---|---|
| all + ways | = | always | all + most | = | almost |
| all + ready | = | already | all + together | = | altogether |
| all + though | = | although | all + so | = | also |

**RULE - 8 : When *ly* is added to a word ending in *y*, its *y* becomes *i*, as:**

| | | | | | |
|---|---|---|---|---|---|
| hearty + ly | = | heartily | speedy + ly | = | speedily |
| haughty + ly | = | haughtily | lazy + ly | = | lazily |

**Exception**: sly + ly = slyly

**RULE - 9 : When *ing* is added to a verb ending in *y*, its *y* does not change to *i*, as:**

| | | | | | |
|---|---|---|---|---|---|
| carry + ing | = | carrying | marry + ing | = | marrying |
| cry + ing | = | crying | obey + ing | = | obeying |

**RULE - 10 : When *ing* is added to a verb ending in *ie*, it becomes *y*, as:**

| | | | | | |
|---|---|---|---|---|---|
| die + ing | = | dying | lie + ing | = | lying |

## B – PRONUNCIATION

Pronunciation also has some rules that help us to pronounce words.

**RULE - 1 : *a* preceding the ending *r, ss, sk, ft* and *st* sounds as long *a*:**

| | | | | |
|---|---|---|---|---|
| bar | grass | bask | craft | last |
| car | pass | task | after | fast |

**RULE - 2 : In long words with *our* at the end, *our* sounds as *er*:**

| | | | |
|---|---|---|---|
| colour | favour | humour | glamour |
| honour | labour | rumour | harbour |

**RULE - 3 : In words ending in *mb*, *b* remains silent:**

| | | | | | | | |
|---|---|---|---|---|---|---|---|
| dumb | = | dum | limb | = | lim | climb | = | clime |
| thumb | = | thum | lamb | = | lam | crumb | = | crum |

**RULE - 4 :** **Ending *sure* in a word sounds as *zer* :**

pleasure — *plazer*    treasure — *trazer*    measure — *mazer*

**RULE - 5 :** **Ending *ture* in a word sounds as *cher*:**

nature — na-cher    feature — fea-cher

**RULE - 6 :** ***d* followed by *j* or *g* sounding as *j*, remains silent:**

adjective — ajektive    judge — juj

adjust — ajust    budge — buj

**NOTE :**

1. *Bravo* is pronounced **braavo**
2. *England* is pronounced **ing-lend**
3. *Thomas* is pronounced **Tomus**
4. *Midas* is pronounced **My-das**

## Practice Exercises

I. *Write the correct word in each blank:*

| | | | | |
|---|---|---|---|---|
| (*a*) | write + ing | .................. | tie + ing | .................. |
| | agree + ing | .................. | be + ing | .................. |
| (*b*) | thin + er | .................. | rob + er | .................. |
| | sit + ing | .................. | beg + ing | .................. |
| (*c*) | angry + ly | .................. | sly + ly | .................. |
| | due + ly | .................. | true + ly | .................. |
| (*d*) | hope + full | .................. | thank + full | .................. |
| | die + ing | .................. | all + mighty | .................. |

II. *How will you pronounce the following words?*

| | | | | | | | | |
|---|---|---|---|---|---|---|---|---|
| (a) | tar | ............ | bark | ............ | fast | ............ | spark | ............ |
| (b) | comb | ............ | tomb | ............ | dumb | ............ | limb | ............ |
| (c) | flavour | ............ | glamour | ............ | adjective | ............ | leisure | ............ |

III. *Pronounce these words:*

Bravo ............ England ............ pleasure ............ culture ............

# SECTION IV — WRITTEN COMPOSITION

## A - ESSAY - WRITING

### 1. THE HORSE

**Outline:**

1. *a common tame animal*
2. *body features, food and age*
3. *used for riding, hunting and drawing carriages*
4. *used in wars in the past*
5. *useful, intelligent and faithful*

The horse is a common tame animal. After the cow, buffalo and the goat, it is the most useful tame animal. It is trained for several jobs.

The horse is a four-footed animal. It has undivided hoofs which are very strong. It has no horns on its head. It has a bushy tail and also a mane on its neck. A horse generally lives for 20-25 years. It lives on grass. It is fed with grams and oats too.

The horse is used for riding. Also, it draws our carts and carriages. It is used in hunting as well. In big grasslands, graziers use it while tending their cattle. In the past, horses were used in wars also. The warriors fought on horse-back with swords, etc.

Horse-riding is a good pastime. Horses are used in some games even today. Polo and the obstacle race are two such games.

The horse is a very useful animal indeed. It is very intelligent and agile as well. Above all, it is very faithful.

# 2. MY SCHOOL

**Outine:**

1. *name, location and distance*
2. *building and its parts, playground*
3. *principal, staff and strength*
4. *general*

I read in Modern School. It is a primary school with classes I to V. It is located outside our town by the road-side. It is about a kilometre away from my house. I go to school on foot. It takes me about 15-20 minutes to reach school. Many children come to school by bus.

My school has a grand building with 15 classrooms and a hall. There are the principal's office, the staff-room, a library and the clerk's room. A clean toilet and a water-cooler are also there. A fine garden and grassy lawns are there on one side and a big playground on the other side.

Mrs Thomas is the principal of our school. There are twenty teachers to teach different subjects. There are about 500 pupils in our school. Each class has two sections. Our school uniform consists of a white shirt, blue shorts/skirt, a blue necktie and a blue belt.

Our teachers teach us with love and care. They teach us how to read and write. They teach us proper manners and good habits as well. I respect and obey them. Our school is a very good school. I like my school very much.

# 3. MY DAY

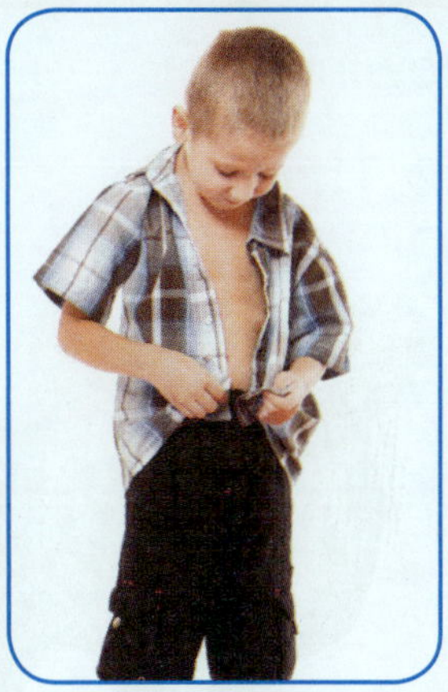

**Outline:**

1. *getting up, walk, toilet, bath, prayer*
2. *dressing up, breakfast, leaving for school*
3. *at school, back home, meal, rest*
4. *homework, play, TV programme*
5. *dinner, stroll, going to bed*

I wake up around 5:00 a.m. and greet everyone at home before heading out for a walk. Coming back, I brush my teeth and ease myself. Then I have my bath and pray to God.

Next, I put on my school dress. The breakfast is ready by now. After having my breakfast, I prepare my bag of books. Then I say goodbye to my parents and leave for school.

At school, I study and play. The school is over at 1:30 p.m. and I return home. Reaching home, I have my lunch and lie down for a short nap.

I get up at about 3:00 p.m. and wash myself. Then I do my homework with my mother's help. When it is over, I go to play with my friends.

I return at about 6:00 p.m. and watch the TV programme. My brothers and sisters are there too. At about 8:00 p.m., we all have dinner. My brother and I, then, have a stroll along the road. When we return, it is 9:30 p.m. I say my bedtime prayer, wish my parents goodnight and go to bed.

# Practice Exercises

Write an essay on each of the following:

(a) 1. The Cow

2. The Camel

3. The Dog

(b) 1. My House

2. My Classroom

(c) My Best Friend

# B - STORY - WRITING

## 1. TWO COCKS AT QUARREL

Once there lived two cocks in a farmyard. Either of them claimed to be the master of the farmyard. So they often quarrelled with each other. One day they had a bitter fight to decide who the master of the farmyard was. When the fight was over, the victor crowed and clapped its wings in great delight.

It made so much noise that an eagle passing by swooped down and carried it away. Now, the entire farmyard belonged to the defeated cock.

**MORAL : GOD'S WILL IS SUPREME.**

# 2. THE CROW AND THE PITCHER

It was a hot summer day. A crow felt very thirsty and flew about hither and thither in search of water. He got very tired and came to a tree.

Suddenly the crow caught sight of a pitcher which had a little water in it.

The crow looked about carefully and saw some pebbles lying near the pitcher. At once, he hit upon an idea. Picking up the pebbles one by one, he dropped them into the pitcher. Soon the water in the pitcher came up. The crow quenched his thirst and flew away.

**MORAL : WHERE THERE IS A WILL, THERE IS A WAY.**

## 3. THE EAGLE AND THE WOODCUTTER

Once a woodcutter saw an eagle that had been caught in a trap. Being kind-hearted by nature, he set the eagle free. The eagle looked at the woodcutter in gratitude and flew away.

Some time later, the woodcutter thought of having his lunch. So he sat down on a rock atop a hill. Just then, the eagle flew down and took away the woodcutter's hat. The woodcutter got up to run after the eagle. As soon as he got away from the rock, it gave way with a crash. As a result, the woodcutter escaped being hurt. The grateful eagle had repaid its well-wisher.

**MORAL : KINDNESS BRINGS ITS OWN REWARD.**

# Practice Exercises

*Expand each outline into a readable story with the help of the pictures:*

1. A lion sleeping under a tree— a mouse comes out of its hole—runs across the body of the sleeping lion—the lion wakes up—catches it in his paw—the mouse prays for mercy—the lion spares its life—some days later, the lion caught in a net—roars aloud—the mouse hears the noise—comes and nibbles the net—the lion gets free.

2. A hungry fox roams in search of food—sees a grove of trees at a distance—goes to the grove—finds a vine of grapes—the grapes hanging very high up—the fox jumps up hard to get at the grapes—cannot reach them—takes rest and again jumps—cannot reach them—feels tired—leaves trying anymore—goes away saying, "These grapes must be very sour."

3. A hungry fox roaming in search of food—finds nothing to eat anywhere—at last comes to a tree—sits under it to take rest—just then a crow reaches there with a piece of meat in its beak—the fox plans to get the piece of meat—greets the crow—praises his voice—requests him to sing a song—the crow caws—the piece of meat comes down—the fox makes a good catch of it.

4. A fox roaming in search of food—falls in a shallow well—tries to come out but cannot —suddenly a goat comes that way—peeps into the well—sees the fox and asks why she is there—the fox replies, "To drink cool water"—asks the goat to come down—the goat taken in—jumps into the well—the fox climbs up its back and comes out.

# C - APPLICATION - WRITING

Small children have to write applications to the principal asking for leave. Let us show you how to do this. An application has four parts:

1. Beginning 2. Salutation 3. Body 4. Ending

**BEGINNING**

It states the rank and address of the person to whom you apply.

*The Principal,*

*Modern School, Auckland.*

**SALUTATION**

It states words of respect for the person applied to, as:

*Sir/Madam*

**BODY**

Starting on the line next to the salutation, it states the application's purpose.

*Most respectfully I beg....................................*

**ENDING**

It forms the closing words—*yours obediently* written on the left/right side of the page with the applicant's name below it.

*Yours obediently,*

*John Smith, III-A.* Date: October 20, 2023

## 1. Leave Due to an Urgent Work

The Principal,
Modern School, Auckland.
Sir,
Most humbly I beg to state that I have an urgent job to do at home. Kindly grant me leave for today, August 25, only.

Yours obediently,
Phil Clare, III-A. Date: August 25, 2023

## 2. Leave Due to Sickness

The Principal,
Modern School, Auckland.

Sir,

Most respectfully I beg to state that I am suffering from fever. Therefore I cannot come to school. Kindly grant me leave for two days — August 25 and 26.

Your most obedient pupil,

Tony Lee, III-B. Date: September 25, 2023

## 3. Leave Due to a Family Function

The Principal,
Modern School, Auckland.

Sir,

Most humbly and respectfully I beg to state that the marriage of my sister falls tomorrow. So I cannot attend school for three days, *i.e.* from April 25 to April 27, 2023. Kindly grant me leave for these three days.

Your most obedient pupil,

Annie D'souza, III-B. Date: April 25 , 2023

# Practice Exercises

1. Write an application to your principal requesting him to grant you leave for two days as you have to attend your brother's wedding celebrations.

2. Write an application to your principal requesting him to grant you leave for two days as you have caught a cold.

3. Write an application to your principal requesting him to grant you leave for one day as you have an urgent piece of work at home.